Crystallization-Study
of the
Psalms

Volume Three

Witness Lee

The Holy Word for Morning Revival

Living Stream Ministry
Anaheim, CA • www.lsm.org

© 2012 Living Stream Ministry

All rights reserved. No part of this work may be reproduced or transmitted in any form or by any means—graphic, electronic, or mechanical, including photocopying, recording, or information storage and retrieval systems—without written permission from the publisher.

First Edition, January 2012.

ISBN 978-0-7363-6110-1

Published by

Living Stream Ministry

2431 W. La Palma Ave., Anaheim, CA 92801 U.S.A.

P. O. Box 2121, Anaheim, CA 92814 U.S.A.

Printed in the United States of America

12 13 14 15 / 5 4 3 2 1

Contents

Week	Title	Page
	Preface	v

2011 Winter Training

CRYSTALLIZATION-STUDY OF THE PSALMS

	Title and Banners	273
13	**The Need for Christ as Our Unique Portion and Desire to Be Properly Appreciated and Exalted by Us**	
	Outline	275
	Day 1	280
14	**The Secret Revelation concerning the Enjoyment of Christ as the Incarnated Triune God, the God-man**	
	Outline	294
	Day 1	300
15	**God's Desire for Zion with Christ**	
	Outline	314
	Day 1	318
16	**The Highest and Fullest Experience of God— Taking God as Our Habitation, Our Eternal Dwelling Place**	
	Outline	333
	Day 1	338

Week	Title	Page

17 **Christ's Eternal and Unchanging Existence in His Resurrection**

    Outline   353
    Day 1   358

18 **The Highest Revelation of Christ**

    Outline   373
    Day 1   378

Recovery Version Reading Schedules:
    Old Testament   392
    New Testament   396

Daily Verse Cards   401

Preface

1. This book is intended as an aid to believers in developing a daily time of morning revival with the Lord in His word. At the same time, it provides a limited review of the winter training held December 26-31, 2011, in Anaheim, California, on the "Crystallization-study of the Psalms." Through intimate contact with the Lord in His word, the believers can be constituted with life and truth and thereby equipped to prophesy in the meetings of the church unto the building up of the Body of Christ.
2. The entire content of this book is taken from the *Crystallization-study Outlines: The Psalms (2)*, the text and footnotes of the Recovery Version of the Bible, selections from the writings of Witness Lee and Watchman Nee, and *Hymns*, all of which are published by Living Stream Ministry.
3. The book is divided into weeks. One training message is covered per week. Each week presents first the message outline, followed by six daily portions, a hymn, and then some space for writing. The training outline has been divided into days, corresponding to the six daily portions. Each daily portion covers certain points and begins with a section entitled "Morning Nourishment." This section contains selected verses and a short reading that can provide rich spiritual nourishment through intimate fellowship with the Lord. The "Morning Nourishment" is followed by a section entitled "Today's Reading," a longer portion of ministry related to the day's main points. Each day's portion concludes with a short list of references for further reading and some space for the saints to make notes concerning their spiritual inspiration, enlightenment, and enjoyment to serve as a reminder of what they have received of the Lord that day.
4. The space provided at the end of each week is for composing a short prophecy. This prophecy can be composed by considering all of our daily notes, the "harvest" of our inspirations during the week, and preparing a main point with

some sub-points to be spoken in the church meetings for the organic building up of the Body of Christ.
5. Following the last week in this volume, we have provided reading schedules for both the Old and New Testaments in the Recovery Version with footnotes. These schedules are arranged so that one can read through both the Old and New Testaments of the Recovery Version with footnotes in two years.
6. As a practical aid to the saints' feeding on the Word throughout the day, we have provided verse cards at the end of the volume, which correspond to each day's scripture reading. These may be cut out and carried along as a source of spiritual enlightenment and nourishment in the saints' daily lives.
7. *Crystallization-study Outlines: The Psalms (2)* was compiled by Living Stream Ministry from the writings of Witness Lee and Watchman Nee. The outlines, footnotes, and cross-references in the Recovery Version of the Bible are by Witness Lee. All of the other references cited in this publication are from the published ministry of Witness Lee and Watchman Nee.

Winter Training
(December 26-31, 2011)

CRYSTALLIZATION-STUDY OF THE PSALMS

Banners:

Whenever God's people exalt Christ,
giving Him the preeminence
in every aspect of their living,
there is restoration and revival.

To take God as our habitation,
our eternal dwelling place,
is the highest and fullest
experience of God.

God's heart is set on Zion,
the city of God, with Christ within it,
and on Zion we have the church
as the Body of Christ
and God's economy for His testimony.

The praise in the Psalms
issues in the consummate praise
with Hallelujahs
because the earth
has been fully recovered by God
and brought under the reign of Christ
with the kingdom.

WEEK 13 — OUTLINE

The Need for Christ as Our Unique Portion and Desire to Be Properly Appreciated and Exalted by Us

Scripture Reading: Psa. 73; 80

Day 1

I. **The intrinsic reason for the desolation of God's house was that Christ was not properly appreciated and exalted by God's people; they did not give Him the preeminence, the first place, in everything (Psa. 74:1-11; 2 Chron. 36:19; Col. 1:18; Rev. 2:4):**

   A. Their failure to give Christ the preeminence and to honor and exalt Him was the cause of their becoming sinful and evil (Jer. 2:13).

   B. The desolation of the church as the house of God always issues from the negligence of the experience of Christ (1 Cor. 1:9-13, 23-24, 30; cf. 3 John 9).

   C. The real revival in the church depends upon everyone in the church life giving Christ the first place in everything (Psa. 73:25; 80:15, 17; cf. Hab. 3:2; Hosea 6:1-3):

   1. To give the Lord the first place in all things is to love Him with the first love, the best love, regarding Him as everything in our life (Rev. 2:4; Col. 1:18; 3:11).

Day 2

   2. We must not love anyone or anything above the Lord, including our soul-life (Matt. 10:37-39; Rev. 12:11).

   3. We love the Lord because He first loved us, infusing His loving essence into us and generating within us the love with which we love Him (1 John 4:19, 7-8, 16):

      a. Christ's love of affection constrains us to live and to die to Him (2 Cor. 5:14-15; Rom. 14:7-9).

      b. Christ's love makes the believers martyrs for Him (Rev. 2:10; 12:11; Rom. 8:35-37).

WEEK 13 — OUTLINE

4. We love the Lord according to the divine dispensing of the Divine Trinity as love (5:5; 8:39, 35; 15:30).
D. The enjoyment of God in the house and city of God can be maintained and preserved only when Christ is properly appreciated and exalted by God's people:
  1. An idol is anything within us that we love more than the Lord and that replaces the Lord in our life (Ezek. 14:3).
  2. Anything, matter, or person that preoccupies us and keeps us from the full enjoyment of Christ is an idol (1 John 5:21).

Day 3 & Day 4

II. **Psalm 73 is on the sufferings of the seeking saints and unveils God, Christ, as our unique portion and desire (1 Cor. 1:2):**
  A. Psalm 73:2-16 records the sufferings and puzzles of the God-seeking psalmist:
    1. The psalmist was nearly stumbled by the situation concerning the prosperity of the wicked (vv. 2-3).
    2. The psalmist said that he had purified his heart in vain and that he had been plagued all day long (vv. 13-14).
    3. If the psalmist had spoken to others about his situation, they would have been stumbled (v. 15).
    4. The more the psalmist considered his situation, trying to understand it, the more he was troubled and perplexed (v. 16).
  B. Through the revelation given in the sanctuary of God, the psalmist obtained the solution to his troubling and perplexing situation (vv. 17-28):
    1. The sanctuary of God is the place where we may obtain the revelation that we need (Lev. 24:2-4; Dan. 2:17-23; cf. 5:12, 14).
    2. God's sanctuary is in our spirit and in the church (1 Cor. 3:16; Eph. 2:22).
    3. We enter into the sanctuary of God by exercising our spirit and living in the church (1 Tim. 4:7; 3:15).

WEEK 13 — OUTLINE

4. Once we are in the sanctuary—in the spirit and in the church—we receive another view, a particular perception (Psa. 73:17-20):
   a. Certain secrets in the Bible were not made known to us until we came into the twofold sanctuary—our spirit as the personal sanctuary and the church as the corporate sanctuary.
   b. God's way is made known in the sanctuary; when we exercise our spirit and live in the church, God's way becomes clear to us (77:13).
C. Psalm 73:25-26 is the revelation given in the sanctuary of God to the suffering and seeking saints:
   1. "Whom do I have in heaven but You? / And besides You there is nothing I desire on earth" (v. 25):
      a. Verse 25 reveals that God's pure seeker would have God as his only possession in heaven and his unique desire on earth:
         1) God was the psalmist's unique goal; the psalmist did not care for anything except God and gaining Him.
         2) In this matter Paul was the same as the psalmist, counting all things as refuse in order to gain Christ (Phil. 3:8).
      b. The psalmist was pure in heart (Psa. 73:1):
         1) To be pure in heart is to have God as our one goal (Matt. 5:8).
         2) A pure heart is one that is set on nothing but God:
            a) God Himself is the reality; anything other than God is vanity.
            b) If we continue to seek something other than God, our heart is set on vanity.
            c) Only a seeker with a pure heart can say that he has nothing but God and desires nothing besides God.

Day 5

WEEK 13 — OUTLINE

2. "My flesh and my heart fail, / But God is the rock of my heart and my portion forever" (Psa. 73:26):
   a. The psalmist realized that God was working to deprive him of all material things so that he might enjoy God in an absolute way:
      1) Through the revelation given in the sanctuary, he learned why God does not allow the seeking saints to prosper as the worldly people do.
      2) God intends that nothing should distract us from the absolute enjoyment of Himself.
      3) God's intention with the seeking saints is to remove all material blessings and physical enjoyments so that they may find everything in God.
   b. When the psalmist went into the sanctuary of God, he received the revelation that nothing in heaven or on earth can be his enjoyment but God Himself, and he took God as his all—the rock of his heart and his portion forever (Deut. 32:4, 15, 18, 30-31; Psa. 18:2, 31, 46; 31:2-3; 61:2; 62:2, 6-7; 71:3; 78:35; 89:26; 92:15; 94:22; 95:1; Matt. 16:18; 1 Cor. 10:4; Eph. 3:17a; Col. 1:12; Eph. 3:8).

Day 6

III. **Psalm 80 reveals that restoration comes by exalting Christ:**
   A. In verses 1 through 7 the psalmist prays that the Shepherd of Israel would give ear (v. 1); in both verses 3 and 7 he prays, "O God, restore us; / And cause Your face to shine, and we will be saved."
   B. In verses 8 through 13 the psalmist speaks regarding God's dealing with Israel as His vine, which He brought out of Egypt and planted; whereas the vine once was flourishing, it eventually became desolate.
   C. In verses 14 through 19 the psalmist asks God to visit His vine (Israel) for the sake of Christ as the man of His right hand:

WEEK 13 — OUTLINE

1. *Son* in verse 15 refers to the Lord Jesus; when He became a man, He joined Himself to Israel—He is "the son whom You have strengthened for Yourself" (Hosea 11:1; Matt. 2:15).
2. In Psalm 80:17 the psalmist goes on to say, "Let Your hand be upon the man of Your right hand, / Upon the son of man whom You have strengthened for Yourself"; this verse reveals that Christ is at the right hand of God, the highest place in the universe; the first place, the highest position, the preeminence, has been given to Christ (Mark 16:19; Acts 2:33; 5:31; Phil. 2:9-11).
3. The way to be restored from desolation is to exalt Christ as the full solution to every problem (1 Cor. 1:9, 24, 30):
   a. Whenever God's people do not give Christ the preeminence, the house of God, signifying the church, becomes desolate.
   b. Whenever God's people exalt Christ, giving Him the preeminence in every aspect of their living, there is restoration and revival (Psa. 80:18-19).
4. Christ is now at the right hand of God (Rom. 8:34; Col. 3:1; 1 Pet. 3:22), and whoever calls upon Him as such a One will be restored and revived (Acts 2:33, 21; Rom. 10:12-13).
5. As regenerated people, we need to come together in the meetings of the church to exalt Christ by praising, singing, and shouting (1 Cor. 14:26):
   a. Instead of being silent, we should exercise our spiritual birthright to exalt Christ.
   b. The more we exalt Christ, giving Him the preeminence in everything, the more we will be revived and restored.

WEEK 13 — DAY 1

Morning Nourishment

Psa. Why, O God, have You cast *us* off forever?...Remem-
74:1-2 ber Your assembly, which You have purchased of old, which You have redeemed *as* the tribe of Your inheritance, *and* Mount Zion, where You dwell.

Jer. For My people have committed two evils: they have
2:13 forsaken Me, the fountain of living waters, to hew out for themselves cisterns, broken cisterns, which hold no water.

[Psalm 74] concerns the desolation of the house of God. After reaching the highest enjoyment of God in His house and His city at the end of Book Two, the psalmist lost this enjoyment, and God's house was desolated, as described in this psalm. Verses 1-11 are the psalmist's painful presentation of the perpetual ruins and damage in the sanctuary of God (v. 3). The temple, God's house, was desolated to such an extent that it was burned (vv. 7-8), and the city surrounding it was ruined (2 Chron. 36:19). The intrinsic reason for the desolation was that Christ was not exalted by God's people; they did not give Him the preeminence, the first place, in everything (Jer. 2:13; cf. Col. 1:18; Rev. 2:4 and footnote 2). The problem of desolation is solved by Christ being properly appreciated and exalted by God's people (see footnote 1 on Psa. 80:17). The enjoyment of God in the house and the city of God can be maintained and preserved only when Christ is properly appreciated and exalted by God's people. (Psa. 74:1, footnote 1)

Today's Reading

What was the cause of the desolation of God's house? Apparently it was because the children of Israel were evil and sinful. However, the intrinsic reason for the desolation was that Christ was not exalted by God's people; they did not give Him the preeminence, the first place, in everything. Actually their failure to give Christ the preeminence, their failure to honor and exalt Him, was the cause of their becoming sinful and evil.

The principle is the same with us in the church life today. If we do not love Christ with our first love, giving Him the first place in everything that He may have the preeminence among us, the church will become desolate. The desolation of the church as the house of God always issues from the negligence of the experience of Christ....The problem of desolation is solved by Christ being properly appreciated and exalted by God's people....If all the saints in [a local church] would give Christ the preeminence, exalting Him to the uttermost and loving Him with the first love, there would be a genuine revival. The real revival in the church depends upon everyone in the church life giving Christ the first place in everything.

[Psalm 74] verses 1 through 11 are the psalmist's painful presentation of the perpetual ruins and damages in the sanctuary of God....Verses [1 and 2] indicate that the psalmist was concerned about two things—God's people and God's dwelling place. Both God's people and His dwelling place had been damaged. Regarding this, the psalmist was deeply disappointed.

Verses 12 through 23 are a desperate cry for God's interest according to His power and based on His covenant. The psalmist did not pray for his own interest—he prayed for God's interest. He cried out to God for God's interest according to His power as described in verses 13 through 17. Then in verse 20 the psalmist said to God, "Regard the covenant." Here he seemed to be saying, "O God, You must regard the covenant which You made with our fathers Abraham, Isaac, and Jacob. You cannot forget it. You may disregard us, for we are evil, but You cannot disregard the covenant which You made."

The psalmist's prayer here is an example of the best kind of prayer—the prayer that is for God's interest, that is according to God's power, and that is based upon God's faithfulness to His covenant. We all need to learn to pray in this way. I believe that God heard this prayer of the psalmist and answered it, for eventually He came in to restore the ruined sanctuary. (*Life-study of the Psalms,* pp. 352-353, 355-356)

Further Reading: Life-study of the Psalms, msg. 30

Enlightenment and inspiration:

WEEK 13 — DAY 2

Morning Nourishment

Rev. 2:4 But I have *one thing* against you, that you have left your first love.

1 John 4:16 And we know and have believed the love which God has in us. God is love, and he who abides in love abides in God and God abides in him.

5:21 Little children, guard yourselves from idols.

The Lord charges us to overcome all kinds of religion, and in these seven epistles [in Revelation 2 and 3] He also charges us to overcome some other matters. The first thing we are charged to overcome is the leaving, the missing, the losing, of the first love (Rev. 2:4-5a).

Our God, our Christ, our Lord, is not only loving but also very affectionate. He is full of affection. God has "fallen in love" with us, His chosen and redeemed people. If you say, "O Lord Jesus, I love You," right away you will fall in love with Him. Quite often I would not do some things, not merely because they are not right or because I fear God but because I love Him. (*The Overcomers*, pp. 30-31)

Today's Reading

We need to overcome the loss of the first love. The church in Ephesus was a good,...an orderly,...and a formal church (Rev. 2:2-3). Surely we would like such a church, but such an orderly church had left the first love (v. 4). The Greek word for *first* is the same as that translated *best* in Luke 15:22. Our first love toward the Lord must be the best love for Him. When the prodigal son in Luke 15 came back home, the father told the servants to bring the *best* robe. The *best* here is the first.

Many Christians think that the first love is the love with which we loved the Lord Jesus when we were saved. I would not say that this is wrong, but it is not adequate. The first love which is the best love is much more than this. The first love is the love which is God Himself. In the Bible we are told that God is love (1 John 4:8, 16). In the whole universe, only God is love. The Lord charges the husbands to love their wives. But it is impossible for the husbands to love their wives in themselves because we are not love. There is only one Person who is love—God.

God is not only the best but also the first. In the whole universe, God is first. Genesis 1:1 says, "In the beginning God...." This is the opening of the Bible. God is the beginning. God is the first. Colossians tells us that our Christ must have the first place. He must have the preeminence (1:18b). Christ must be the first. What is it to recover the first love? To recover the first love is to consider the Lord Jesus as the first in everything. If we make Christ everything in our life, that means we have overcome the loss of the first love.

We also need to overcome in the kind of ties we wear, in the way that we style our hair, and in all of the small things. In all things we should give the preeminence to Christ. If we do this, our Christian life will be different, and our feeling will be different. Throughout the day, we will be happy in the Lord. When we are joyful in and with the Lord, everything is pleasant....The enjoyment of the Lord as grace is with those who love Him (Eph. 6:24)....The leaving of the first love is the source of and main reason for the failure of the church throughout the ages. (*The Overcomers,* pp. 31-33)

There are many idols among God's people today. These idols preoccupy them and keep them from the enjoyment of Christ. It is possible for almost anything to be an idol to us....Many Christians are fully occupied by things, matters, and persons other than Christ. As an example of these occupations, I would refer to talking on the telephone. Some saints claim that they are too busy to pray. However, they have much time to spend talking on the telephone. For them, talking on the telephone has become an idol. An idol is anything that keeps us from the enjoyment of Christ as our good land. (*Life-study of Exodus,* p. 1893)

Further Reading: The Overcomers, chs. 2-3; *The Collected Works of Watchman Nee,* vol. 11, pp. 731-753; *Life-study of Exodus,* msg. 178

Enlightenment and inspiration: _____

WEEK 13 — DAY 3

Morning Nourishment

Psa. When I considered this in order to understand *it*,
73:16-17 it was a troublesome task in my sight, until I went into the sanctuary of God...
25-26 Whom do I have in heaven *but You?* And besides You there is nothing I desire on earth. My flesh and my heart fail, *but* God is the rock of my heart and my portion forever.

Psalm 73:1 tells us that God is good to those who are pure in heart. To be pure in heart is to have God as our one goal and aim. No doubt the psalmist here was this kind of person.

Verses 2 through 16 are a record of the sufferings and puzzles of the God-seeking psalmist. Verse 2 says, "As for me, my feet were nearly turned aside;/My steps had almost slipped." This indicates that the psalmist was nearly stumbled by the situation concerning the prosperity of the wicked (vv. 3-12). Whereas Psalm 1 says that the wicked do not prosper, here the psalmist is puzzled by the prosperity of the wicked, who are at ease and heap up riches (v. 12). The psalmist goes on to say that he has purified his heart in vain, that he has been plagued all day long, and that he was chastened every morning (vv. 13-14). Psalm 1 says that the one who keeps the law will be blessed, but in Psalm 73 we see a law-keeper who was plagued. In verse 15 the psalmist continues, "If I had said, I will speak thus;/Behold, I would have betrayed the generation of Your children." This pious seeker of God was suffering, but if he had told others about his situation, they would have been stumbled...[because] here is one who kept the law, yet was not at all prosperous. In [verse 16] the psalmist tells us that he was puzzled....The more the psalmist considered the situation, the more he was troubled and puzzled. (*Life-study of the Psalms*, pp. 353-354)

Today's Reading

In Psalm 73 verses 17 through 28 we see that the psalmist obtained the solution in the sanctuary of God....Where is God's sanctuary today? First, God's sanctuary, His habitation, is in our spirit. Second, God's sanctuary is the church. Thus, to go into the sanctuary of God, we need to turn to our spirit and then go to the meetings of the church. Once we are in the sanctuary—in the spirit and in the church—we will have another view, a particular perception, of the situation concerning the wicked.

Having gone into the sanctuary of God, the psalmist could perceive that the wicked were set in slippery places to be cast down into ruins (v. 18). This caused the psalmist to say, "How they are made desolate in a moment! / They are utterly consumed by terrors. / Like a dream, when one awakes, You, O Lord, / Upon arising, will despise their image" (vv. 19-20).

[Verse 25] reveals that God's pure seeker would have God as his only possession in heaven and his unique desire on earth. God was the psalmist's unique goal. The psalmist did not care for anything except God and gaining Him. In this matter, Paul was the same. In Philippians 3:8 Paul said that he counted all things as refuse in order to gain Christ. Psalm 73 ends with these words: "My flesh and my heart fail, / But God is the rock of my heart and my portion forever" (v. 26). Here we have the answer to the psalmist's question concerning his suffering and the prosperity of the wicked. The one who does not care for God may gain many things and seem to prosper. However, the one who cares for God will be restricted by God and even stripped by God of many things....This is what happened to Job.

[Psalm 77 says that] God's way is hidden in the sea, and His paths in the great waters with His footsteps are not known to men (v. 19), but His way is revealed in His sanctuary (v. 13). The thought here is similar to that in Psalm 73 where the psalmist, puzzled by the prosperity of the wicked and the suffering of the seeking saints, said, "When I considered this in order to understand it, / It was a troublesome task in my sight, / Until I went into the sanctuary of God; / Then I perceived their end" (vv. 16-17). In the sanctuary, the psalmist had a clear view of the situation. (*Life-study of the Psalms*, pp. 354-355, 361-362)

Further Reading: Life-study of the Psalms, msg. 31

Enlightenment and inspiration: _____

_____
_____

WEEK 13 — DAY 4

Morning Nourishment

Psa. 73:28 But as for me, drawing near to God is good for me; I have made the Lord Jehovah my refuge, that I may declare all Your works.

77:13 O God, Your way is in the sanctuary; who is so great a god as God?

Eph. 2:22 In whom you also are being built together into a dwelling place of God in spirit.

Spiritually speaking, for us today God's sanctuary is our spirit and the church. Many Christians neglect the matter of the spirit. Some do not even realize that they have a human spirit. Likewise, many do not have a proper understanding concerning the church. Without paying attention to our spirit and to the church, we cannot know God's way, which is revealed in His sanctuary. I thank the Lord that we in the Lord's recovery know both the spirit and the church....Today we have a twofold sanctuary: a private sanctuary—the spirit—and a public sanctuary—the church. Many of us can testify that certain secrets in the Bible were unknown to us until we went into this twofold sanctuary. When we exercise our spirit and live in the church, God's way becomes clear to us.

In the early years of my ministry, I would give many principles to those who consulted with me about whom they should marry. I discovered, however, that this did not work, and eventually I changed my practice regarding this. Now if young people ask me concerning marriage, I will not give them any principles; instead, I will encourage them to exercise their spirit and to attend the meetings of the church. If those who are concerned about marriage will enter into the sanctuary of God by exercising their spirit and living in the church, they will know what they should do. The main point in Psalm 77 is that God's way is revealed in His sanctuary. (*Life-study of the Psalms*, p. 362)

Today's Reading

Both the sunlight and the moonlight are natural light for us to observe natural things, such as mountains, rivers, flowers, grass, trees, and wild beasts. However, natural light cannot help us to know God's administration, God's economy, and God's eternal purpose. To know God's administration and economy, we must have the light of the golden lampstand. When we enter into the realm of God's presence, there is no light without the golden lampstand. Outside of the realm of God's presence, we have sunlight and moonlight, and we have the natural view, but we can never have the view of God's economy and administration.

I hope that we will practice using the phrase *the light of the Holy Place*. The light of the golden lampstand is the light of the Holy Place, not the light of the sky, nor that of the sun, the moon, or anything natural. The light of the Holy Place is from the burning of the olive oil in the golden lampstand. The Holy Place today is the church. The church is the lampstand, and it is also the Holy Place....In Psalm 73, the psalmist saw a situation which puzzled him and was difficult to comprehend. The more he looked at it, the more it was unclear to him; the more he analyzed it, the more it did not make sense and the more he became befuddled. Eventually, he said, "When I considered this in order to understand it, / It was a troublesome task in my sight, / Until I went into the sanctuary of God; / Then I perceived their end" (vv. 16-17). This shows us that when he went into the sanctuary, the Holy Place, he understood.

Once we go into the Holy Place, we understand. This is because in the Holy Place is the throne, the One who sits on the throne, and the presence of God, and before the throne of God is the shining of the seven burning lamps of fire. Once we enter into this realm, immediately we are clear. We know God's eternal purpose, His heart's intention, and His economy, and we also know which path we should take for the journey before us. This is due to the light in the Holy Place. (*The Ultimate Significance of the Golden Lampstand,* pp. 45, 48, 50)

Further Reading: The Ultimate Significance of the Golden Lampstand, ch. 4

Enlightenment and inspiration: _____

WEEK 13 — DAY 5

Morning Nourishment

Psa. Surely God is good to Israel, to those who are pure
73:1 in heart.
   13 Surely I have purified my heart in vain, and I have washed my hands in innocence.
Matt. Blessed are the pure in heart, for they shall see God.
5:8

Let us look briefly at Psalm 24 in the light of Psalm 73. Psalm 24:1 says, "The earth is Jehovah's," and verse 3 asks, "Who may ascend the mountain of Jehovah?" Verse 4 answers: "He who has clean hands and a pure heart, / Who has not lifted up his soul to falsehood / Or sworn deceitfully." Some may think that this verse refers to those who keep the law. But if we read Psalm 73, we have these very matters mentioned [in verse 13]....Vanity is anything beside God. Idols are vanity; worldly prosperity is vanity; anything but God is vanity. A pure heart is one that is set on nothing but God. Only one who has a pure heart can say, "Whom do I have in heaven but You? / And besides You there is nothing I desire on earth" [v. 25]. If you are still seeking anything other than God, your heart is set upon vanity. God Himself is the reality. Do not imagine that Psalm 24:4 signifies the keeping of the law. Not at all. It refers to one whose heart is set upon nothing but God. The one in Psalm 24:4 is the one in Psalm 73. This is the one who has washed his hands and purified his heart. He has a pure heart....Psalm 24:4 refers not to the law-keepers but to the God-seekers. "Who may ascend the mountain of Jehovah?" The God-seekers! (*Christ and the Church Revealed and Typified in the Psalms*, p. 135)

Today's Reading

The sanctuary of God is the place where we may obtain the revelation we need. The sanctuary here undoubtedly signifies the dwelling place of God. Our spirit today is God's dwelling place. Even more, the local churches are God's dwelling place. Hence, we must turn to our spirit, and we must turn to the local church; then we will be clear. Our spirit and the local church are the places where we receive divine revelation, where we obtain the explanation to all our problems. When "I went into the sanctuary of God; / Then I perceived…" [Psa. 73:17].

What did he perceive?…He realized that God was working to deprive him of all material things so that he might enjoy God in such an absolute way. This is the revelation. Why do the wicked prosper and their riches continually increase? It is because God has given them up; He simply lets them go on their own way. They have nothing whatever to do with the enjoyment of God. But God's intention with the seeking saints is to remove all material blessings and all physical enjoyments in order that they may find everything in God. Nothing in heaven or on earth can be their enjoyment but God Himself. It was by the psalmist's experience, as recorded in the first part of Psalm 73, that he…received revelation. He learned why God would not allow the seeking saints to prosper as the worldlings do. God intends that nothing should distract us from the absolute enjoyment of Himself. Eventually, it is not a matter of merely keeping the law, but of seeking God absolutely. It is not a matter of doing good or evil, right or wrong—if you are concerned about that, you are still occupied with the tree of the knowledge of good and evil. It is a matter of seeking God, obtaining God, possessing God. It is a matter of experiencing God to the extent that you also can say,…"I do not care for anything but the tree of life; I do not care for anything other than God Himself." This is Psalm 73. When the psalmist went into the sanctuary of God, he received this revelation and took God Himself as his all.… [For us to have this experience] we must be in the spirit and in the local church, the sanctuary of God. Just by this one psalm we may see the difference between Book Three and Book One. There is a great improvement. It is not a matter of keeping the law or of being right or wrong, but of having God and of keeping God as everything. (*Christ and the Church Revealed and Typified in the Psalms,* pp. 133-134)

Further Reading: Christ and the Church Revealed and Typified in the Psalms, chs. 12-13

Enlightenment and inspiration: _____
_____
_____

WEEK 13 — DAY 6

Morning Nourishment

Psa. 80:1, 3 O Shepherd of Israel, give ear, You who lead Joseph like a flock; You who are enthroned *between* the cherubim, shine forth....O God, restore us; and cause Your face to shine, and we will be saved.

14-15 O God of hosts, turn, we beseech You; look down from heaven and see, and visit this vine, even the stock which Your right hand has planted and the son whom You have strengthened for Yourself.

In Psalm 80:1-7 we have the psalmist's prayer for Israel as God's flock. The psalmist prayed that the Shepherd of Israel would give ear (v. 1). In both verse 3 and verse 7, he prayed, "O God, restore us; / And cause Your face to shine, and we will be saved."

In verses 8 through 13 the psalmist speaks regarding God's dealing with Israel as His vine, which He brought out of Egypt and planted. Whereas the vine once was flourishing, it eventually became desolate. (*Life-study of the Psalms*, p. 364)

Today's Reading

In [Psalm 80:] 14-19 the psalmist asks God to visit His vine for the sake of Christ as the Man of His right hand....The vine which God had brought out of Egypt and planted in the good land became evil, and God took away its protection. As a result, Israel became a prey to the Gentile powers, such as Babylon. However, among the Israelites there is one—the Lord Jesus—who is signified by the word "son" in verse 15. Hosea 11:1 indicates that when Christ became a man, He, the Son of God, joined Himself to Israel. He is "the son whom You have strengthened for Yourself" (Psa. 80:15). During the time Israel was forsaken by God, this unique One was strengthened by God for Himself.

In verse 17 the psalmist goes on to say, "Let Your hand be upon the man of Your right hand, / Upon the son of man whom You have strengthened for Yourself." From this verse we see that Christ is at the right hand of God, the highest place in the universe. This reveals that the first place, the highest position, the preeminence, has been given to Christ. This is the exaltation of Christ.

The way of restoration is the exaltation of Christ. Whenever God's people exalt Christ, there will be restoration and revival. We can have revival among us only if we exalt Christ, letting Him have the preeminence and giving Him the first place in everything. If a church is somewhat cold and old and desires revival, that church should give Christ the preeminence, recognizing Him as the One who is at the right hand of God. Christ is now at the right hand of God, and whoever calls upon Him as such a One will be restored and revived. In our private life, married life, family life, and church life, Christ needs to be at the right hand of God. If He is exalted in every aspect of our living, there will be restoration everywhere. Exalting Christ is the way for revival, for restoration.

The day is coming when Israel will be restored through their exalting of Christ. When they repent to Christ and give Him the first place, they will be restored.

According to Psalm 80, the vine is Israel and the man at God's right hand is Christ. The world rejected Christ and put Him on the cross, but God came in to raise Him from among the dead and to seat Him at God's right hand in the heavens. Today, as we visit people for the preaching of the gospel, we need to tell them that Christ, the Son of God, became a man, died on the cross for their sins, resurrected, and ascended to the right hand of God in the heavens, and now they need to call upon Him. In the sight of God, for a sinner to call upon the Lord Jesus is to exalt Him. When a sinner exalts Christ by calling upon Him, that sinner will be regenerated.

As regenerated people we need to come together in the meetings of the church to exalt Christ by praising, singing, and shouting. Instead of being silent, we should exercise our spiritual birthright to exalt Christ. We should declare, "Lord Jesus, You are at the right hand of God. You have the preeminence in my private life, married life, family life, and church life." The more we exalt Christ, giving Him the preeminence in everything, the more we will be revived and restored. (*Life-study of the Psalms,* pp. 364-365)

Further Reading: Life-study of the Psalms, msg. 31

Enlightenment and inspiration: _____

WEEK 13 — HYMN

Hymns, #1225

1. Lord, to know Thee as the Body,
   Is my desperate need today,
   Oh, to see Thee in Thy members,
   'Tis for this I long and pray.
   No more just to know Thy headship,
   In an individual way,
   But to see Thee incarnated,
   As the Body-Christ, I pray.

2. Through the years, Thy saints have sought Thee,
   Longing for reality;
   Gazing upward, searching inward,
   Thirsting for the sight of Thee.
   Now reveal that Christ in heaven,
   Is the Body manifest;
   And the Christ who dwells within us
   As the Body is expressed.

3. Prone to be misled, I know it,
   By my lofty thoughts of Thee,
   Easy 'tis for self to seek Thee,
   Yet not touch reality,
   Oh, how much I need to find Thee,
   In Thy members here below.
   God eternal dwells among us,
   Manifest in flesh to know.

4. Limit, Lord, my independence,
   Let me to Thy Body turn;
   Not just seeking light from heaven,
   But the church's sense to learn.
   May we be the stones for building,
   Not the formless, useless clay,
   Gain in us Thy heart's desire,
   Corporately Thyself display.

WEEK 13 — PROPHECY

Composition for prophecy with main point and sub-points:

WEEK 14 — OUTLINE

*The Secret Revelation concerning
the Enjoyment of Christ
as the Incarnated Triune God, the God-man*

Scripture Reading: Psa. 84

Day 1
I. **The deeper love and sweeter experience of the house of God in Psalm 84 come after the experience of God's dealing and stripping and are recovered by the experience of God as our unique portion and by Christ being given the unique position (vv. 1-12; 73:17, 25-26; 80:15, 17; Col. 1:17a, 18b):**

   A. God's purpose in dealing with His holy people is that they would be emptied of everything to receive only God as their gain and be rebuilt with the Divine Trinity to become the masterpiece of God, fulfilling God's eternal economy for His expression (Job 10:13; Eph. 3:9-11; 2:10).

   B. God is faithful to take away all our idols and to lead us into His economy for us to enjoy Christ so that He may have a recovery purely and wholly of the person of Christ (1 Cor. 1:9; 1 John 5:21; cf. Jer. 2:13; Lam. 3:22-24).

Day 2
II. **The intrinsic content of Psalm 84 is the secret revelation concerning the enjoyment of Christ as the incarnated Triune God, the God-man (Col. 2:9; 1:12):**

   A. The center of this secret revelation is the house of God (Psa. 84:4, 10a), typified by the tabernacle (Exo. 40:2-8) and by the temple (1 Kings 6:1-3; 8:3-11).

   B. Christ as the embodiment of the Triune God (Col. 2:9) is the fulfillment of the types of the tabernacle and the temple:

      1. This fulfillment commenced in His incarnation as the individual Christ (John 1:14; 2:21) and will continue (1 Tim. 3:15-16) until it consummates in the New Jerusalem as the corporate Christ, the great God-man (Rev. 21:2-3, 22).

2. The New Testament, from Matthew through Revelation, covers the entire span of the incarnation of the Triune God and is a record of the divine incarnation.
3. The enjoyment of Christ as the incarnated Triune God in God's house is portrayed by the arrangement of the tabernacle and its furnishings (see diagram on page 297).

III. The psalmist's longing and even fainting to be in God's tabernacles indicates to what extent the psalmist loved God's tabernacles; this love was matured through many trials (Psa. 84:2).

IV. "At Your two altars even the sparrow has found a home; / And the swallow, a nest for herself, / Where she may lay her young, / O Jehovah of hosts, my King and my God" (v. 3):
  A. The two altars—the bronze altar for the sacrifices and the golden altar of incense—signify the leading consummations of the work of the incarnated Triune God, who is Christ as the embodiment of God for His increase (Exo. 40:5-6):
    1. At the bronze altar, a type of the cross of Christ, our problems before God are solved through the crucified Christ as the sacrifices; this qualifies us to enter into the tabernacle, a type of Christ as the incarnated and enterable Triune God, and to contact God at the incense altar (the bronze altar for the sacrifices is related to God's judicial redemption accomplished by Christ in His earthly ministry) (Rom. 5:10a; 8:3; Heb. 9:14; 7:27; 10:10).
    2. At the golden altar of incense in front of the Holy of Holies (9:4), the resurrected Christ in His ascension is the incense for us to be accepted by God in peace; through our prayer at the incense altar we enter into the Holy of Holies—our spirit—where we experience Christ as the Ark of the Testimony with its contents (the golden altar of incense is related to God's

organic salvation carried out by Christ in His heavenly ministry) (Rom. 8:34; Heb. 7:25; 9:24; 10:19).

3. Through such an experience of Christ we are incorporated into the tabernacle, the incarnated Triune God, to become a part of the corporate Christ (1 Cor. 12:12) as God's testimony for His manifestation.

B. Through these two altars God's redeemed, the "sparrows" and "swallows," can find a nest as their refuge and a home with God in rest (cf. Psa. 90:1; 91:1):

1. The cross of Christ, typified by the bronze altar, is our "nest," our refuge, where we are saved from our troubles and where we "lay" our young, that is, produce new believers through the preaching of the gospel.

2. When we experience the resurrected Christ in His ascension, typified by the golden altar of incense, we are accepted by God in such a Christ and find a home, a place of rest, in the house of God.

3. This house is the processed and consummated Triune God united, mingled, and incorporated with all His redeemed, regenerated, and transformed elect (John 14:1-23) to be the Body of Christ in the present age and the New Jerusalem as the mutual dwelling place of God and His redeemed in eternity (Rev. 21:3, 22).

Day 4
V. "Blessed are those who dwell in Your house; / They will yet be praising You. Selah... / O Jehovah of hosts, blessed is the man / Who trusts in You" (Psa. 84:4, 12):

A. In type, the house is the church as a totality (1 Tim. 3:15), and the tabernacles (Psa. 84:1) are the local churches (Rev. 1:11).

B. Praising the Lord should be our living, and our church life should be a life of praising (Psa. 22:3; 50:23; 1 Thes. 5:16-19; Phil. 4:4, 11-13).

WEEK 14 — OUTLINE

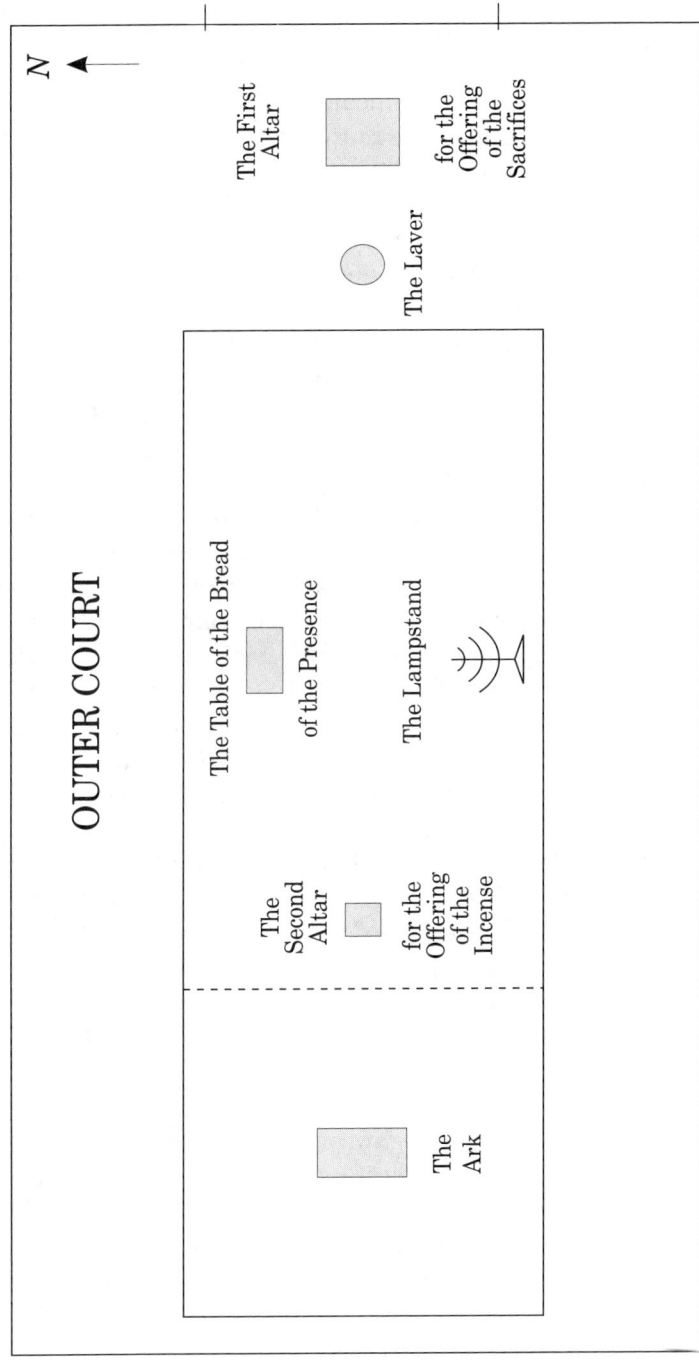

WEEK 14 — OUTLINE

C. In the church life we trust in God, not in ourselves or in our natural human ability to work out a solution to our difficult situations (2 Cor. 1:8-9, 12).

VI. **"Blessed is the man whose strength is in You, / In whose heart are the highways to Zion" (Psa. 84:5; cf. Phil. 4:13; John 15:5):**

A. The highways to Zion signify our intention to enter into the church as the house of God and are the blessed highways for seeking the incarnated Triune God in His consummations, typified by the furniture in the tabernacle (Heb. 10:19-22).

B. On the one hand, we have entered into God; on the other hand, we are still on the highways to enter into God.

C. That the highways to Zion are in our heart means that we need to take the way of the church internally, not merely externally; when we are deeply in the inner life, we will certainly be in the way of the church; the highways to Zion will be within our heart (cf. 1 John 1:3-4).

D. Zion is the very spot where God is, the Holy of Holies; the overcomers become Zion, and the Lord's recovery is to build up Zion (Rev. 21:16; cf. Exo. 26:2-8; 1 Kings 6:20; Rev. 2:7).

Day 5 VII. **"Passing through the valley of Baca, / They make it a spring; / Indeed the early rain covers it with blessings" (Psa. 84:6):**

A. *Baca* means "weeping"; on the one hand, those on the highways to Zion are strengthened in God (v. 5); on the other hand, they are opposed by Satan, who causes them to suffer persecution.

B. The trouble and persecution caused by Satan can make the highways a valley of weeping; this special term indicates that the psalmist had been disciplined by God and had been stripped by Him.

C. The highways to Zion are not external, superficial, or cheap; we must pay a price to take the way of the church (Phil. 3:7-8; Matt. 25:9; Rev. 3:18; Acts 20:19, 31; Psa. 56:8).

WEEK 14 — OUTLINE

D. When we pass through the valley of Baca, God makes this valley a spring (cf. Col. 1:24; Heb. 10:34); this spring is the Spirit (John 4:14; 7:38-39).
E. The more we weep on the highways to Zion, the more we receive the Spirit; while we are weeping, we are being filled with the Spirit, and the Spirit becomes our spring.
F. Those who come into the church life by passing through the valley of weeping find that this weeping eventually becomes a great blessing to them; this blessing is the Spirit.
G. The tears they shed are their own, but these tears issue in a spring, which becomes the early rain, the Spirit as the blessing (Zech. 10:1; Gal. 3:14; Eph. 1:3).

Day 6 VIII. **"They go from strength to strength; / Each appears before God in Zion... / For a day in Your courts is better than a thousand; / I would rather stand at the threshold of the house of my God / Than dwell in the tents of the wicked. / For Jehovah God is a sun and a shield; / Jehovah gives grace and glory" (Psa. 84:7, 10-11a):**

A. The more we go on in the church life, the more strength we will gain (cf. Prov. 4:18; 2 Cor. 3:18).
B. If our service is intrinsically according to God's will in the church life, each day will be worth many days in God's eyes (Joel 2:25a).
C. The blessings of our dwelling in the house of God are our enjoyment of the incarnated and consummated Triune God as our sun to supply us with life (John 1:4; 8:12), as our shield to protect us from God's enemy (Eph. 6:11-17), as grace for our inward enjoyment (John 1:14, 17), and as glory for the outward manifestation of God in splendor (Rev. 21:11, 23).

WEEK 14 — DAY 1

Morning Nourishment

Job 10:13 But You have hidden these things in Your heart; I know that this is with You.

Eph. 3:9 And to enlighten all *that they may see* what the economy of the mystery is, which throughout the ages has been hidden in God, who created all things.

Psa. 84:6 Passing through the valley of Baca, they make it a spring; indeed the early rain covers it with blessings.

In Book Three...the three leading psalms [are] Psalms 73, 80, and 84. In Psalm 73 we have seen how we need God as our unique portion, and in Psalm 80 we have seen how Christ must have the unique position. When these are secured, we have, in Psalm 84, the sweeter experience of the house of God. The house becomes much sweeter than before the desolation. It has been recovered by the experience of God as our unique portion and by Christ being given the unique position. (*Christ and the Church Revealed and Typified in the Psalms*, p. 161)

Today's Reading

Psalm 84 comes after a number of psalms on God's dealing and stripping....For example, the psalmist in Psalm 73 was puzzled by God's dealing and stripping and did not become clear concerning this until he entered into the sanctuary of God. The situation of the psalmists in such psalms was nearly the same as Job's....[In Psalm 84:6] the valley of Baca is the valley of weeping. This special term indicates that the psalmist had been dealt with by God and had been stripped by Him. (*Life-study of the Psalms*, p. 369)

The subject of Job is the purpose of God's dealing with His holy one....[It] is a book of the debates of godly men concerning the purpose of the sufferings of the saints. However,...[Job] could not tell us what the purpose of God's dealing was. For this we need to read Paul's Epistles. Paul tells us that the purpose of our sufferings is that God wants to strip us of all things that we may gain God.

Ethically speaking, Job was very good....God boasted to Satan regarding how good Job was (1:8; 2:3), but only God knew that Job was short of God. Because of Job's need and His loving concern for

Job, God held a council in the heavens with the angels to talk about Job. Although it is doubtful that Satan was invited, [he] attended that council. Satan was condemned by God and even sentenced by God (Isa. 14:15; Ezek. 28:15-19), yet in His wisdom and sovereignty God did not execute His judgment over Satan....Satan was the unique one in the whole universe who would fulfill God's intention of stripping Job of his possessions and his ethical attainment.

Satan's evil concept concerning God's dealing with His seeking people is based on his commercial principle of gain or loss. He does not know that God's purpose in dealing with His lovers, even in the way of loss, is that they may gain Him to the fullest extent, that God might be expressed through them for the fulfillment of the purpose in His creation of man. Job lost all that he had, but ultimately he gained God Himself. God stripped his all in order that He could be his all for his full transformation and conformation to the glorious image of God in His Son (Rom. 8:29). (*The Holy Word for Morning Revival: Job,* p. 14)

First Corinthians 1:9 says that God is faithful in calling us into the fellowship of His Son,...but He may not seem to be faithful in the matter of caring for our welfare. God's faithfulness is not according to our natural understanding. When we believed in the Lord Jesus, we might have expected to have peace and blessing; but instead, we might have had many troubles and might have lost our security, our health, or our possessions....Our peace, safety, health, and possessions may become idols to us, and God is faithful to take these things away so that we might drink of Him as the fountain of living waters. God is faithful in leading us into His economy, and His economy is for us to enjoy Christ, to absorb Christ, to drink Christ, to eat Christ, and to assimilate Christ that God may increase in us to fulfill His economy. (*The Holy Word for Morning Revival: Jeremiah,* pp. 6-7)

Further Reading: Christ and the Church Revealed and Typified in the Psalms, ch. 15; *The Holy Word for Morning Revival: Job,* pp. 14-19; *The Holy Word for Morning Revival: Jeremiah,* pp. 6-7

Enlightenment and inspiration:

WEEK 14 — DAY 2

Morning Nourishment

Psa. **How lovely are Your tabernacles**, O Jehovah of
84:1-4 hosts! My soul longs, indeed even faints, for the courts of Jehovah....At Your *two* altars even the sparrow has found a home....Blessed are those who dwell in Your house...

In Psalm 84 there is a secret revelation concerning our enjoyment of the incarnated Triune God....In this Christ we have God the Father, God the Son, and God the Spirit. The Father, the Son, and the Spirit coexist and also coinhere, that is, they dwell in one another. The Father is in the Son, and the Son is in the Father. The Father and the Son are in the Spirit, and the Spirit is in the Father and in the Son....Furthermore, in Christ the Triune God has passed through a long process to become the processed and consummated Triune God. This is Christ as our enjoyment and as our portion allotted to us by God (Col. 1:12).

The center of this secret revelation is the house of God (Psa. 84:4, 10a), typified by the tabernacle (Exo. 40:2-8) and by the temple (1 Kings 6:1-3; 8:3-11). Both of these types have been fulfilled in Christ. (*Life-study of the Psalms*, p. 381)

Today's Reading

The diagram [on page 297] shows us that in the outer court there are two items: the first altar, the bronze altar, for the offering of the sacrifices, and the laver, a large basin containing water for washing. At the first altar, all of our problems before God are solved through the sacrifices, and we are saved. Why, then, do we still need the laver?...We need to see that God's goal is not to solve our problems; God's goal is to make us, the old creation, the new creation. In order to become the new creation, we need to be washed. Our old creation was made of the dust of the earth, and this dust needs to be washed away in the laver....After we have experienced the altar and the laver, we are qualified to enter into the incarnated God, signified by the tabernacle.

In the Old Testament no one could enter into God. But in His incarnation God has become enterable. However, many of today's

Christians, not realizing that God is enterable, do not proceed from the first altar to the laver, and they do not enter into God. They may speak of fearing God, of exalting God, and of loving God but not of entering into God.

Our enterable God is Christ, the God-man, the incarnated Triune God and the embodiment of the Triune God. When we enter into Him, we have the showbread table for the life supply and the lampstand for the light of life. This enables us to live and walk in the incarnated Triune God.

In the incarnated Triune God we have not only the showbread table and the lampstand but also the second altar, the incense altar, for the offering of the incense. The incense signifies Christ as our acceptance. At the first altar our problems before God are solved through Christ as the sacrifices. At the second altar Christ is the incense for us to be accepted by God.

According to the Old Testament, the incense altar was in front of the Ark of the Testimony. But there was a veil separating the incense altar in the Holy Place from the Ark of the Testimony in the Holy of Holies (Exo. 26:31-35). However, through the death of Christ this veil has been rent (Matt. 27:51; Heb. 10:20). Now there is no longer a separation between the incense altar and the Ark of the Testimony. They are one. This indicates that when we are accepted by God in Christ as our acceptance, we become God's testimony to express, to manifest, God.

Christ as the embodiment of the Triune God (Col. 2:9) is the fulfillment of the types of the tabernacle and the temple. This fulfillment commenced in His incarnation (John 1:14; 2:21) and will consummate in the New Jerusalem (Rev. 21:2-3). The New Testament, from Matthew 1 through Revelation 22, covers the entire span of the incarnation of the Triune God....The individual Christ is the beginning of the incarnation of the Triune God and...the corporate Christ, the New Jerusalem, will be the conclusion and consummation. (*Life-study of the Psalms*, pp. 383-384)

Further Reading: *Life-study of the Psalms*, msg. 33

Enlightenment and inspiration:

WEEK 14 — DAY 3

Morning Nourishment

Psa. 84:3 At Your *two* altars even the sparrow has found a home; and the swallow, a nest for herself, where she may lay her young…

Exo. 40:5-6 And you shall put the golden altar for incense before the Ark of the Testimony and set up the screen of the entrance to the tabernacle. And you shall put the altar of burnt offering before the entrance of the tabernacle of the Tent of Meeting.

The two altars signify the leading consummations of the work of the incarnated Triune God, who is Christ as the embodiment of God for His increase. The mentioning of these two altars together in Exodus 40:5-6 indicates that they are closely related in our spiritual experience. At the bronze altar, a type of the cross of Christ, our problems before God are solved through the crucified Christ as the sacrifices. This qualifies us to enter into the tabernacle, a type of Christ as the incarnated and enterable Triune God, and to contact God at the incense altar. At the golden altar of incense in front of the Holy of Holies…the resurrected Christ in His ascension is the incense for us to be accepted by God in peace. Through our prayer at the incense altar we enter into the Holy of Holies—our spirit (Heb. 10:19)—where we experience Christ as the Ark of the Testimony with its contents. Through such an experience of Christ we are incorporated into the tabernacle, the incarnated Triune God, to become a part of the corporate Christ (1 Cor. 12:12) as God's testimony for His manifestation. (Psa. 84:3, footnote 1)

Today's Reading

A home is a place of rest, and a nest is a place of refuge.…The cross of Christ, typified by the bronze altar, is our "nest," our refuge, where we are saved from our troubles and where we "lay" our young, that is, produce new believers through the preaching of the gospel. When we experience the resurrected Christ in His ascension, typified by the golden altar of incense, we are accepted by God in such a Christ and find a home, a place of rest, in the house of God. This house is the processed and consummated

Triune God united, mingled, and incorporated with all His redeemed, regenerated, and transformed elect (John 14:1-23) to be the Body of Christ in the present age and the New Jerusalem as the mutual dwelling place of God and His redeemed in eternity (Rev. 21:3, 22). (Psa. 84:3, footnote 3)

Through these two altars God's redeemed can find their home with God in rest....For us today, the brass altar is a refuge. We hide ourselves under the cross, escaping our troubles, and thus we are covered and have refuge. Then at the golden altar we contact our Christ in the heavens. This contact is not for refuge—it is for rest.

A swallow is small and weak and is troubled by storms and by many other things. But a swallow has a nest, a refuge. Like a swallow coming to the nest where she may lay her young, we may come to the cross of Christ as our refuge. Here we may bring our "young," those whom we contact in our preaching of the gospel. Spiritually speaking, at the "nest" of the cross we should "lay" our young, our spiritual children....To do this we need to bring sinners to the cross of Christ. It is here, at the cross, that we have our nest, our refuge, and it is here that we "lay our young," that is, produce our spiritual children. Before contacting the cross they were sinners, but by contacting the cross they become believers, young children in the Lord. As we teach our young to call on the Lord, they will learn to offer prayer to God at the altar of incense. Then in their experience these two altars will be closely related.

As we experience these two altars in the church, we can say with Paul, "I did not determine to know anything among you except Jesus Christ, and this One crucified" (1 Cor. 2:2). We know only Christ and His cross. The cross is our refuge, our hiding place, and Christ Himself is our acceptance. Day by day we come to these two altars. Day by day we are hiding and resting. We come to the cross, where we have refuge, and we come to Christ, where we rest and are at home. (*Life-study of the Psalms*, pp. 371-373)

Further Reading: Life-study of the Psalms, msg. 32

Enlightenment and inspiration: _____

WEEK 14 — DAY 4

Morning Nourishment

Psa. Blessed are those who dwell in Your house; they
84:4-5 will yet be praising You. Selah. Blessed is the man whose strength is in You, in whose heart are the highways *to* Zion.
7 They go from strength to strength; *each* appears before God in Zion.

In type, the house is the church as a totality (1 Tim. 3:15), and the tabernacles (v. 1) are the local churches (Rev. 1:11). (Psa. 84:4, footnote 1)

The highways to Zion signify our intention to enter into the church as the house of God and to seek the incarnated Triune God in His consummations, typified by the furniture in the tabernacle....On the one hand, we have entered into God; on the other hand, we are still on the highways to enter into God. That the highways are in our heart means that we need to take the way of the church internally, not merely externally. (Psa. 84:5, footnote 1)

To dwell in God's house is to praise Him. Quite often, however, we are lacking in praise. Our vital groups should be full of praising. Not to praise the Lord is to be dormant, but to praise Him is to be vital. Praising the Lord should be our living, and our church life should be a life of praising. (*Life-study of the Psalms*, p. 373)

Today's Reading

Psalm 84:5 tells us that the one is blessed in whose heart are the highways to Zion. The highways to Zion are the blessed highways for seeking the incarnated Triune God in His consummations (comprising the washing laver, the showbread table, the lampstand, and the Ark of the Testimony). From our spiritual experiences we have learned that, on the one hand, we have entered into God, but, on the other hand, we are still on the way to enter into God. None of us can say that our entering into God has been completed. For many of us, the entering into God has only begun. We are in God, yet we are still on the highways to enter into God.

On the highways to Zion we have strength in God. Many of us can testify that before we came into the church we were weak and hesitant, but once we made the decision to come to the church, we were strengthened in God. (*Life-study of the Psalms,* pp. 385, 374)

Today in the church age, the God-men who were perfected and matured are Zion, the overcomers, the vital groups within the churches. But in the new heaven and new earth, there will be no more Zion, only Jerusalem, because all the unqualified saints will have been qualified to be Zion. In other words, the entire New Jerusalem will become Zion. What is Zion? Zion is the very spot where God is, that is, the Holy of Holies. In Revelation 21 there is a sign signifying that the New Jerusalem will be the Holy of Holies. Its dimensions are the dimensions of a cube, twelve thousand stadia long, twelve thousand stadia wide, and twelve thousand stadia high (v. 16). That is the Holy of Holies, because the Holy of Holies in the Old Testament in both the tabernacle and the temple was a cube, equal in length, breadth, and height (Exo. 26:2-8; 1 Kings 6:20).

By that time all the God-redeemed people will be transformed, not only to be the same as God in life and nature, but also to be the same in God's appearance. Revelation 4 tells us that God looks like jasper (v. 3). Then Revelation 21 says that the entire New Jerusalem has the appearance of jasper (v. 11). Thus, God's redeemed people have become absolutely the very God in life, in nature, and in appearance, but not in His Godhead.

What shall we do in the light of this revelation? There is no other way to reach this high peak except by praying. It is more than evident that Jerusalem is here as a big realm of Christians, but where is Zion, the overcomers? In the book of Revelation what the Lord wants and what the Lord will build up is Zion, the overcomers. The overcomers are the very Zion, where God is. This is the intrinsic reality of the spiritual revelation in the holy Word of God. We have to realize what the Lord's recovery is. The Lord's recovery is to build up Zion. (*The Practical Points concerning Blending,* pp. 45-47)

Further Reading: The Practical Points concerning Blending, ch. 5

Enlightenment and inspiration: _____

WEEK 14 — DAY 5

Morning Nourishment

Psa. 84:6-7 Passing through the valley of Baca, they make it a spring; indeed the early rain covers it with blessings. They go from strength to strength; *each* appears before God in Zion.

Heb. 12:22 But you have come forward to Mount Zion and to the city of the living God, the heavenly Jerusalem; and to myriads of angels, to the universal gathering.

[handwritten: 23 - And to the church of the firstborn...]

Psalm 84:6a speaks of passing through the valley of Baca.... "Baca" means "weeping." On the one hand, when we had the intention to come into the church life, we were strengthened in God; on the other hand, we were opposed by Satan, who has caused many saints to suffer persecution. The trouble and persecution caused by Satan can make our highway a valley of weeping.

When we pass through the valley of Baca, God makes this valley a spring (v. 6b). If we take the highway to go to God's house, trouble and persecution will come to us, and such things will cause us to weep. But God will turn our tears into a spring. Only those who weep will have a spring. The more tears we shed, the greater will be the spring. (*Life-study of the Psalms*, pp. 374-375)

Today's Reading

Psalm 84:6c says, "Indeed the early rain covers it with blessings." According to our experience, this means that our tears become a spring and that this spring becomes the early rain that covers the valley with blessings. This early rain is the Spirit, and the Spirit is our blessing....A certain brother,...before he believed in the Lord Jesus,...was a Moslem. After he was saved and came into the church life, he suffered a great deal of persecution...[that] nearly killed him, and he shed many tears. But those tears became a spring; the spring became the Spirit as the early rain; and as a result this brother was very living. Those who come into the church life by passing through the valley of weeping will find that this weeping eventually becomes a great blessing to them. This blessing is the Spirit. The tears they shed are their own, but these tears become a spring, which becomes the early rain, the Spirit as the blessing.

"Strength to strength" (v. 7a)…indicates that strength is added to strength. Those who take the highway to Zion already have strength in God, and now they are strengthened further and thus go from strength to strength.… "Each appears before God in Zion" (v. 7b). The issue of the foregoing is that we appear before God in Zion. We treasure God's habitation because Zion is here. We treasure the church life because here we are in Zion. Even though we are on earth, we are nonetheless in the heavenly Zion (Heb. 12:22). (*Life-study of the Psalms,* p. 375)

[Strictly-speaking Psalm 84:6] does not say that *God* makes it a spring, but that *we* make it such.…Whether the valley of weeping is a place of blessing or not depends wholly on us, not on God. If you take the church way, at a certain point you will encounter many trials and troubles. If you turn away, you will find yourself in a real valley of weeping. But if you are faithful at any cost, if you say, "Lord, even at the cost of my life, I will still go on," you will make the valley of weeping a spring.…I have seen many who, in spite of all the trials, have still gone on in the church. I can testify that their weeping was transformed into blessing. The tears were transformed into springs, into rain which covered the valley with blessings.…It depends upon your attitude. When the church is good and everything is fine, we may praise the Lord.…Sometimes the brothers may not be so lovable.…Sometimes the co-workers may not be so pleasant to you. Sometimes the meetings may not be so living.…Will you quit, will you turn away?…Sometimes the local church may not seem as good as the denominations. Will you go back? Be careful; it all depends upon you. It is not God's responsibility. It is yours. It is not God who makes the valley of weeping a place of blessing; it is you. (*Christ and the Church Revealed and Typified in the Psalms,* pp. 155-156)

Further Reading: Christ and the Church Revealed and Typified in the Psalms, ch. 14

Enlightenment and inspiration: _____

WEEK 14 — DAY 6

Morning Nourishment

Psa. 84:10-12 For a day in Your courts is better than a thousand; I would rather stand at the threshold of the house of my God than dwell in the tents of the wicked. For Jehovah God is a sun and a shield; Jehovah gives grace and glory; He does not withhold anything good from those who walk uprightly. O Jehovah of hosts, blessed is the man who trusts in You.

Psalm 84 bears four aspects. The first aspect is the loveliness of the house of God (v. 1). The second aspect is the longing of the psalmist to enter into God's house (v. 2). Third, there is the aspect of the highways to the house of God (v. 5b). The fourth aspect consists of the blessings of dwelling in the house of God to enjoy God as the sun, the shield, the grace, and the glory. In such a house we enjoy the incarnated and consummated Triune God as our sun to supply us with life, as our shield to protect us from God's enemy, as grace for our enjoyment, and as glory for the manifestation of God. Let us now consider this psalm in more detail.

[In verse 10] the psalmist speaks of one who stands at the threshold, which is the dividing line between the inside and the outside. I surely would like to be one who stands at the threshold of the house of God….It is better to stand at this threshold than to dwell in the tents of the wicked. However, we should not be satisfied to stay at the threshold of the house of God but should enter into His house. (*Life-study of the Psalms*, pp. 380-381, 374, 386)

Today's Reading

"Behold our shield, O God; / And look upon the face of Your anointed" (Psa. 84:9). The "shield" in this verse refers to David the king, and the "anointed" refers also to David the king, typifying Christ. Here the psalmist prayed concerning David, saying that he was the shield to protect them and that he was God's anointed. In typology, however, this anointed one, is Christ. In our prayer we may say, "O God, look upon the face of Christ, Your anointed One, who is our Savior."

The sun [in verse 11] is the source of light, and light gives life. Plants, animals, and human beings all need sunlight in order to live and grow. In our spiritual life, we also need sunlight, and for this we have Christ as our source of light and life....The psalmist goes on to say that Jehovah gives grace and glory with nothing good withheld. Grace and glory are both God Himself. Grace is God for our enjoyment, and glory is God for our splendor. Therefore, in these verses Jehovah God in Christ is four things to us: the shield, the sun, the grace, and the glory.

Psalm 84 was written according to the psalmist's background, which was very similar to Job's background. In verse 11c the psalmist says that God "does not withhold anything good / From those who walk uprightly." In verse 12 he goes on to declare, "O Jehovah of hosts, blessed is the man / Who trusts in You." In verse 11d "those who walk uprightly" probably refers, in the complex sentiments of the psalmist, to those who keep the law. In verse 12 "the man who trusts in You" probably refers, also in the complex sentiments of the psalmist, to the man who dwells in God's house....Such sentiments were not according to God's revelation. Job walked uprightly, yet God not only withheld something from him but also stripped him and consumed him. Furthermore, Job trusted in God, yet he did not always have God's blessing. Do you believe that it is because we walk uprightly that we today enjoy Christ as our sun, shield, grace, and glory? Do you believe that it is because we trust in God that He blesses us? We must confess that in ourselves we cannot walk uprightly or have a firm trust in God.

In type, Psalm 84 shows us how excellent the church life is and how we should treasure it. Here we enjoy the cross of Christ, and here we enjoy Christ Himself. We all should take the highway to come to the church and then dwell here. Here we enjoy our David, our anointed One, our Christ, who is our sun, our shield, our grace, and our glory. (*Life-study of the Psalms,* pp. 376-377)

Further Reading: Life-study of the Psalms, msg. 33

Enlightenment and inspiration: _____
_____
_____

Hymns, #851

1. How lovely is Thy dwelling-place!
   Within Thy courts I long to be;
   Thy presence, Lord, my spirit craves,
   For this my heart cries out to Thee.

2. At Thy burnt-offering altar, Lord,
   And at Thine incense altar blest,
   Even the sparrow finds a home,
   And swallow there prepares her nest.

3. Men, as the sparrow, frail and small,
   When living in Thy house find rest,
   Relying on the altar's blood,
   Enjoying there the incense blest.

4. How blessed are those men indeed!
   Trusting in Thee they are made strong;
   Highways to Zion in their hearts,
   The way they care not, rough or long.

5. Passing the weeping valley they
   Make it a place of springing wells;
   The rain with blessings covers it
   And in the way God's mercy tells.

6. From strength to strength they go, and all
   Before the Lord in Zion meet;
   Thus ever seeking Thine own self,
   They need Thy care and grace replete.

7. Better a day within Thy courts
   Than days a thousand I would tell;
   I'd rather at Thy threshold stand
   Than in the wicked's tents to dwell.

8. Thou art a sun, Thou art a shield,
   Thou grace and glory wilt supply;
   Thy presence and Thy very self
   My need in fulness satisfy.

9. Not one good thing wilt Thou withhold
   From those who walk in uprightness;
   Bless'd is the man that trusts in Thee
   With grace and glory measureless.

WEEK 14 — PROPHECY

Composition for prophecy with main point and sub-points: _____

✱ Stripping / Dealing ⇒ for God to be everything to us
   ⇓
to enter into His house
   ⇓
that our experience may become lovely — our entering into
the "tabernacle / temple"   } Col
   ⇓   ⇓   2:9
John 1:14   Sm 2:21

WEEK 15 — OUTLINE

God's Desire for Zion with Christ

Scripture Reading: Psa. 87; 2:6; 48:1-2

Day 1
I. **Psalm 87 reveals that God's heart is set on Zion, the city of God, with Christ within it (vv. 2-3):**
   A. Zion is central in God's heart (2:6; 48:1-2; 50:2; 99:2; 132:13; 135:21).
   B. Restoration, salvation, and release from sufferings are the desires of the saints, but God's desire is for Zion with His Christ (85:4; 86:2; 88:1-3; 87:2-3):
      1. Salvation is not for ourselves—salvation is for God's purpose and economy.
      2. God saves people for His Christ, for His house, and for Zion, the city of God, in order that one day He might gain the entire earth through Christ with His overcomers (51:18; Eph. 2:4-6, 8, 10, 21-22; Rev. 11:15).

II. **"His foundation is in the holy mountains" (Psa. 87:1):**
   A. This divine foundation, typifying Christ as God's unique foundation for the building up of His house, the church, is built in the "holy mountains," which typify the local churches (1 Cor. 3:11).
   B. As the Christ and the Son of the living God, the Lord Jesus is the unique foundation laid by God for His building (Matt. 16:16, 18; 1 Cor. 3:11).

Day 2
   C. According to Paul's word in 1 Corinthians 3, Christ is a living foundation, a foundation that grows:
      1. God gives the growth, and to give growth is a matter of growing Christ; the Christ who grows within us is a living, growing foundation (vv. 6-7, 11).
      2. The foundation grows in us, and this growth produces gold, silver, and precious stones for the building up of the church (v. 12a).
   D. As Christ, the unique foundation, holds and supports God's building, He dispenses Himself into every part of the building, imparting His element into all the believers (Col. 2:19).

WEEK 15 — OUTLINE

III. "Jehovah loves the gates of Zion" (Psa. 87:2a):
   A. Gates are for coming in and going out, signifying fellowship (1 Cor. 1:9).
   B. Fellowship is related to oneness; fellowship brings all the members of the Body of Christ into oneness (10:16-17; Eph. 4:3-6):
      1. The fellowship among the churches is the fellowship of the body of Christ (1 Cor. 10:16).
      2. Fellowship is the reality of living in the Body of Christ (12:12-13, 27).
   C. The fact that the New Jerusalem has twelve gates indicates that God's holy city will be full of fellowship (Rev. 21:12, 21).

Day 3
IV. "Glorious things are spoken of you, / O city of God" (Psa. 87:3):
   A. Zion is a poetic title of the church in both the universal sense and the local sense (v. 2).
   B. Zion was the city of King David (2 Sam. 5:7), the center of the city of Jerusalem as God's dwelling place on earth:
      1. Zion within Jerusalem typifies the body of overcomers, the perfected and matured God-men, within the church as the heavenly Jerusalem (Heb. 12:22; Rev. 14:1-5).
      2. As the highlight and beauty of the holy city Jerusalem, Zion typifies the overcomers as the high peak, the center, the uplifting, the strengthening, the enriching, the beauty, and the reality of the church (Psa. 48:1-2, 11-12; 50:2; 20:2; 53:6a; 87:2).
      3. The overcomers as Zion are the reality of the Body of Christ and consummate the building up of the Body in the local churches to bring in the consummated holy city, New Jerusalem, the Holy of Holies as God's dwelling place, in eternity (Rev. 21:1-3, 16, 22).
   C. For the Lord to do good in His good pleasure unto Zion is for Him to build up the church, fill the church with His glory, and grant the church His

WEEK 15 — OUTLINE

rich presence with Himself as joy, peace, life, light, security, and every spiritual blessing (Psa. 51:18; cf. Eph. 1:3).

D. Although the Lord has the right, the title, to the earth, today the earth is usurped by His enemy; yet on this usurped earth there is the mountain of Jehovah, Mount Zion, which is absolutely open to the Lord and absolutely possessed by Him (Psa. 24:1-3, 7-10; 2:6; 87:3).

E. In the new heaven and new earth the entire New Jerusalem will become Zion, with all the believers as overcomers (Rev. 14:1; 21:1-2, 16).

Day 4

V. "But of Zion it will be said, / This one and that one were born in her, / And the Most High Himself will establish her. / Jehovah will count / When He records the peoples: / This One was born there" (Psa. 87:5-6):

A. In verses 5 and 6 God's intention is to make a contrast, a comparison, of all other places with Zion.

B. Psalm 87 unveils Christ with all the saints to be God's house for God's city and for God to gain the whole earth (27:4; 36:8-9; 48:1-2; 72:8).

C. *This One* in 87:6 and *this one* and *that one* in verse 5 indicate that Christ Himself and all the saints were born in the heavenly Zion (Matt. 1:20; Gal. 4:26-31; Heb. 12:22-23a).

D. *This One* is the unique One, Christ, who is the totality of all the saints (Psa. 87:5) as the One who is all the saints and in all the saints (Col. 3:11).

Day 5

E. In resurrection God begot a Son, Jesus Christ, and in resurrection God regenerated many sons; this shows us that the resurrection of Christ was a great delivery (Acts 13:33; Rom. 1:3-4; John 20:17; 1 Pet. 1:3):

1. Christ was born as the Firstborn, and we were regenerated as His many brothers, the many sons of God; hence, that birth in resurrection was a corporate birth—the birth of the firstborn Son and His many brothers (Rom. 8:29; Heb. 1:6; 2:10-11).

2. The birth of a new corporate child comprising Christ and His believers was the birth of the new man (Col. 3:10):
   a. The corporate man brought forth by Christ's work in His resurrection is the new man spoken of in Ephesians 2:15.
   b. The Head is the firstborn Son of God, and the Body is a composition of all the many sons of God, the many brothers of the Lord (1:22-23).
   c. This child, this corporate new man, was brought forth through Christ's work in resurrection (John 16:20-22).

VI. "All my springs are in you" (Psa. 87:7b):
   A. *You* is the city of God; all the springs are in Zion.
   B. The processed Triune God is the fountain, the springs, and the river of water of life; the Father is the fountain, the Son is the springs, and the Spirit is the river of water of life (John 4:14; 7:38; Isa. 12:2-3).
   C. In eternity the Lamb will shepherd God's redeemed and guide them to springs of waters of life (Rev. 7:17):
      1. As our Shepherd, Christ will lead us into Himself as the springs of water of life so that we may enjoy the eternal dispensing of the Triune God.
      2. *Springs of waters of life* refers to the unique water of life in different aspects (v. 17; John 7:38; Rev. 22:1).
      3. In the New Jerusalem, the eternal Mount Zion, we will drink of many springs and enjoy many different waters; for eternity we will be able to declare, "All my springs are in you."

WEEK 15 — DAY 1

Morning Nourishment

Psa. His foundation is in the holy mountains. Jehovah
87:1-3 loves the gates of Zion more than all the dwellings of Jacob. Glorious things are spoken of you, O city of God. Selah

In Psalm 85 the saints ask God for restoration, and in Psalm 86 for salvation; but in Psalm 87 we see that God's heart is set on Zion, His city, with Christ within it. Zion here refers not only to the house but to the house with the city....[God's] desire, His heart, is set upon Zion with Christ within it. It is indeed significant that preceding Psalm 87 are Psalms 85 and 86. In Psalm 85 the psalmist says, "Restore us, O God" (v. 4). Psalm 85 is a prayer for restoration. In Psalm 86 the psalmist says, "Save Your servant who trusts in You, O You who are my God" (v. 2). Psalm 86 is a prayer for salvation. These are the desires of the saints, but God's desire is not for these things. His desire is for Zion with His Christ. (*Christ and the Church Revealed and Typified in the Psalms*, pp. 161-162)

Today's Reading

Today we are the same as the psalmists: we are continually desiring restoration and salvation. God would say to us, "Do not be like that. I am for Zion; I am for the church. If you allow Me to have My church, no problem will exist regarding your restoration. If you allow Me to have My church, nothing can withhold any kind of deliverance, any kind of salvation." The church is the real restoration, the real salvation, the real deliverance. In Psalm 87 we see how Zion is central in God's heart. (*Christ and the Church Revealed and Typified in the Psalms*, p. 162)

Throughout the centuries, God's people have been praying for revival, for corporate restoration. God's people have also been concerned about personal salvation, not only from eternal perdition but also from various bothering and entangling things in their daily life. Furthermore, all Christians pray about their sufferings, asking God to release them from their sufferings. In our eyes these three matters are positive, but in God's eyes they are not positive.

Psalm 89 is a lengthy psalm revealing that God cares for nothing other than Christ as the unique Possessor of the whole earth. We, however, regard certain spiritual things—restoration, personal salvation, release from suffering—as very positive. But if we neglect Christ, we will suffer a great loss. Our seeking and our praying will not touch God's heart because God's heart is for Christ with Zion, in which are many saints and which is for the house of God and the city of God for Christ to possess the whole earth.

God's desire is for this Christ who was born in Zion with so many saints for God's house and God's city so that Christ might gain the whole earth. This is God's economy. God does not care for restoration, salvation, and release from suffering as we do. God does not care for our kind of restoration or for the kind of salvation that we seek for ourselves. God saves people for His economy. God saves people for His Christ, for His Zion, and for His house and His city in order that one day He might gain the entire earth through Christ with His overcomers. God is for this.

Psalm 87 firstly refers to Zion's foundation, which is called "His [God's] foundation" (v. 1). This divine foundation, typifying Christ as God's unique foundation for the building up of His house, the church (1 Cor. 3:11), is built in the "holy mountains," which typify the local churches. Jerusalem was built on these holy mountains, and among these mountains the highest peak is the one on which Zion was built, which typifies the church. (*Life-study of the Psalms,* pp. 389, 391, 394-395)

In [1 Corinthians] 3:11 Paul says, "For another foundation no one is able to lay besides that which is laid, which is Jesus Christ." As the Christ and the Son of the living God, the Lord Jesus Christ is the unique foundation laid by God for the building of the church (Matt. 16:16-18). No one can lay any other foundation. (*Life-study of 1 Corinthians,* p. 41)

Further Reading: Life-study of the Psalms, msg. 34; *Christ and the Church Revealed and Typified in the Psalms,* ch. 18

Enlightenment and inspiration: _____

WEEK 15 — DAY 2

Morning Nourishment

1 Cor. For another foundation no one is able to lay besides
3:11 that which is laid, which is Jesus Christ.
1:9 God is faithful, through whom you were called into the fellowship of His Son, Jesus Christ our Lord.

Christ is a living foundation, a foundation that grows....Paul says that he planted, that Apollos watered, and that God gives the growth [1 Cor. 3:6]. To give the growth is a matter of growing Christ. The Christ who grows within us is the unique foundation. Hence, it is a living, growing foundation.

As the foundation grows in us, this growth produces gold, silver, and precious stones, the materials needed for the building up of the church. This is to experience Christ, to enjoy Christ, and to partake of Christ so that we may be transformed for the building. In this way we have the precious materials for the building up of the Body. This is to live Christ for the church. (*Life-study of 2 Corinthians*, pp. 136-137)

Today's Reading

[The] foundation [of a meeting hall] holds and supports the entire building. In the same way, Christ as a living foundation holds and supports the entire church. While He is holding and supporting, He is dispensing and imparting His divine element of life into all the members. The physical foundation of a building cannot impart anything, but Christ as the living foundation is imparting while He is holding and supporting all of us. (*The Economy and Dispensing of God*, p. 76)

Gates [in Psalm 87:2] are for coming in and going out, signifying fellowship. The fact that the New Jerusalem will have twelve gates (Rev. 21:12, 21) indicates that God's holy city will be full of fellowship. (Psa. 87:2, footnote 1)

Fellowship is related to oneness. Just as the circulation of blood in the human body causes all the members of the body to be one, so the fellowship of the divine life in the Body of Christ causes the Body to be one. If any member of our physical body does not participate adequately in the circulation of blood in the body, that member will become unhealthy....The principle is the same with the fellowship of the Body of Christ. All those who believe in Christ Jesus, who have received Him as Redeemer, Savior, and life supply, have the divine life. This divine life...circulates within all of us. This circulation of the divine life in the Body brings all the members of the Body into oneness. This oneness is called the oneness of the Spirit; it is also the oneness of the Body. As long as we have the divine life flowing within us, we are in...the oneness of the Body, the oneness among all the saints. This oneness includes not only the believers but also the Triune God. This is the fellowship among the churches. *(The Conclusion of the New Testament,* p. 2178)

This divine fellowship not only corrects us; it also molds us and even reconstitutes us. This fellowship brings the divine constituent into our spiritual being, causing a change in our being....The divine fellowship is the reality of living in the Body of Christ. The Lord has been frustrated throughout the centuries because of the lack of fellowship. In Revelation 22:20 the Lord Jesus said, "I come quickly," but it has been nearly two thousand years, and the Lord is still not back. The reason is that the believers are individualistic, independent, opinionated, and divisive. The Roman Catholic Church controlled people by its organization, but those who broke away from Catholicism brought in division after division. The believers seem to be like horses without bridles. Today nothing seems to control them. Actually, the divine fellowship should control the believers. The one thing which should rule us is the divine fellowship....By being restricted in this fellowship, the Body of Christ is kept in oneness, and the work of the ministry continues to go on. When we are out of fellowship, everything is finished. The thing which makes everything alive is fellowship. If we learn to fellowship, we will receive many benefits, especially in the Lord's work. *(The Triune God to Be Life to the Tripartite Man,* pp. 147-148)

Further Reading: The Conclusion of the New Testament, msg. 203; *The Triune God to Be Life to the Tripartite Man,* msg. 17

Enlightenment and inspiration: _____

Morning Nourishment

Psa. 48:1-2 Great is Jehovah, and much to be praised in the city of our God, in His holy mountain. Beautiful in elevation, the joy of the whole earth, is Mount Zion, the sides of the north, the city of the great King.

Whereas Psalm 85 is on the seeking of the sons of Korah for restoration and Psalm 86 is on the seeking of David for salvation, Psalm 87 is on the desire of God for Zion with Christ....Zion always implies God's house and God's city. "Zion" is a poetic title of the church in the universal sense and also in the local sense (Heb. 12:22; Gal. 4:26). Therefore, Zion signifies the church universally and locally. The heavenly Zion is the final resting place of the overcomers (Rev. 14:1).

Recently, for the sake of fellowship among the churches, the Lord has led us to practice the clustering and the blending. However, some saints care only for the jurisdiction of their local church, and they do not want anyone to come to them and touch anything related to their local church. This means that they close the gate. In Brother Nee's words, they make their local church a "native church" and a "small empire." This is not Zion, for Zion has many gates for fellowship. (*Life-study of the Psalms*, p. 391)

Today's Reading

Zion was the city of King David (2 Sam. 5:7), the center of the city of Jerusalem, where the temple as God's dwelling place on earth was built (Psa. 9:11; 74:2; 76:2b; 135:21; Isa. 8:18). Zion within Jerusalem typifies the body of overcomers, the perfected and matured God-men, within the church as the heavenly Jerusalem (Heb. 12:22; Rev. 14:1-5). As the highlight and beauty of the holy city Jerusalem (Psa. 48:2; 50:2), Zion typifies the overcomers as the high peak, the center, the uplifting, the strengthening, the enriching, the beauty, and the reality of the church (48:2, 11-12; 20:2; 53:6a; 87:2). The overcomers as Zion are the reality of the Body of Christ and consummate the building up of the Body in the local churches to bring in the consummated holy city, New

WEEK 15 — DAY 3

Jerusalem, the Holy of Holies as God's dwelling place, in eternity (Rev. 21:1-3, 16, 22). In the new heaven and new earth the entire New Jerusalem will become Zion, with all the believers as overcomers (Rev. 21:7 and note 1). (Psalm 48:2, footnote 1)

[Psalm 51:18-19 signifies] the participation in the enjoyment of God in the local church as God's house, God's dwelling, and in the universal church as God's city, God's kingdom, through the all-inclusive Christ as the offerings. If we are those who repent, confess our sins, and ask God for His purging (1 John 1:9), we will have the enjoyment of God in Christ in His house, the local church, and in His city, the universal church. This enjoyment, as the "good" mentioned here, includes God's building up the church, His filling the church with His glory, and His granting the church His rich presence with Himself as joy, peace, life, light, security, and every spiritual blessing (cf. Eph. 1:3). (Psa. 51:18, footnote 1)

The mountain [in Psalm 24:3] implies the city (see Psa. 48:1, footnote 2), which signifies the kingdom of God (cf. 30:7 and footnote). Although the Lord has the right, the title, to the earth (v. 1), today the earth is usurped by His enemy. Yet on this usurped earth there is the mountain of Jehovah, Mount Zion (2:6), which is absolutely open to the Lord and absolutely possessed by Him (vv. 1, 3, 7-10). The overcomers, who are typified by Zion (see footnote 1 on Psa. 48:2), are the beachhead through which the Lord will return to possess the whole earth (Dan. 2:34-35). (Psa. 24:3, footnote 2)

The mountain of Zion was one hundred percent possessed by the Lord, though the entire earth was not. We may express it this way: the earth is the Lord's, yet only the mountain of Zion was actually possessed by the Lord. Likewise, Los Angeles is the Lord's, but only the mountain of the local church is possessed today by the Lord. (*Christ and the Church Revealed and Typified in the Psalms*, p. 56)

Further Reading: Life-study of the Psalms, msg. 22; The Organic Union in God's Relationship with Man, ch. 4

Enlightenment and inspiration: _____

WEEK 15 — DAY 4

Morning Nourishment

Psa. But of Zion it will be said, This one and that one were
87:5-6 born in her, and the Most High Himself will establish her. Jehovah will count when He records the peoples: this One was born there. Selah

[Psalm 87:4-6 is] written poetically....God's intention is to make a contrast, a comparison, of all other places with Zion. In verse 2 God declares that He loves the gates of Zion. But besides Zion on this earth there are many other places...but none of them can compare with Zion. (*Christ and the Church Revealed and Typified in the Psalms*, p. 163)

Today's Reading

Psalm 87 unveils Christ with all the saints to be God's house for God's city and for God to gain the whole earth....[In verse 5] the word about "this one" and "that one" being born in Zion indicates that Zion is full of saints. Verse 6 tells us that "this One"—Christ, the unique One—was born there. Christ Himself and all the saints were born in Zion.

In addition to those born in Zion, Psalm 87 speaks of people born in five other places: Rahab, Babylon, Philistia, Tyre, and Cush. "Rahab" is a poetic title given to Egypt. In the Bible Egypt stands for a place rich in resources, a place where it is easy for one to make a living and where it is possible for one to make a fortune for his enjoyment. When there was a famine in Canaan and people were short of food, they went down to Egypt, a land of riches signifying today's world.

Babylon was famous in the realm of human success and glory. It was the continuation of Babel, where man endeavored to glorify himself by building a tower to heaven. Nebuchadnezzar, king of Babylon, built a great and powerful empire, a monument to man's success and glory.

Philistia was very close to the holy land....When the Ark of God was captured and brought into their country, they devised a way to deal with it. Having contacted the holy land and having learned about the holy things from the holy land, the Philistines became adept in handling holy things according to human wisdom. Today there are many people who are not in the holy things but are very close to these things and have their human way to handle them.

According to the Bible and to history, Tyre was a commercial country of merchandise and of high civilization. Their traffic in commerce was their glory. There are many "Tyres" on earth today.

The last place was Cush (Ethiopia). Cush was a place from which people came to learn of the holy land. The queen of Sheba, for example, came from Ethiopia to learn of Solomon. The Ethiopian eunuch in Acts 8 also came to the holy land to learn. Hence, in history, Cush, or Ethiopia, also had a name and a reputation.

The people from these five places represent all the people on earth....[They] boasted of their "giants," saying, "This one was born there" (v. 4b). Egypt could say that the Pharaohs were born there, and Babylon could say that Nebuchadnezzar was born there. But what does God say concerning Zion? He declares, "This one and that one were born in her." Moses, Joshua, David, Elijah, Peter, Paul, Luther, Calvin, Wesley, Zinzendorf, Darby, Watchman Nee, and so many others were born in Zion. Eventually, even the unique One, Christ, who is the totality of all the saints as the One who is all the saints and in all the saints (Col. 3:11), was born there. This is God's counting, God's record, regarding Zion.

Not all the saints born in Zion are famous ones. Rather, among the singers and the dancers (Psa. 87:7a), there are many unknown ones. We today may be the unknown ones, but we can sing and praise the Lord, saying of Zion, the city of God, "All my springs are in you" [v. 7b]. Let Egypt boast of the Nile and let Babylon boast of the Euphrates. They do not have the springs, but we in Zion have them. (*Life-study of the Psalms,* pp. 392-393)

Further Reading: Life-study of Galatians, msg. 24; *The Conclusion of the New Testament,* msgs. 254-255

Enlightenment and inspiration: _____

WEEK 15 — DAY 5

Morning Nourishment

Acts 13:33 That God has fully fulfilled this *promise* to us their children in raising up Jesus, as it is also written in the second Psalm, "You are My Son; this day have I begotten You."

Rom. 8:29 Because those whom He foreknew, He also predestinated *to be* conformed to the image of His Son, that He might be the Firstborn among many brothers.

When did the Triune God beget His many children?...In the resurrection of Christ. This resurrection was a great birth, a great delivery. In that great delivery in resurrection, Jesus, who was already the only begotten Son of God from eternity (John 1:18; 3:16), was begotten to be the firstborn Son of God among many brothers (Acts 13:33; Rom. 8:29). Now the Triune God has millions and millions of children. In resurrection Jesus is the firstborn Son of God, and we are His many brothers. The firstborn Son and His many brothers were all delivered on the same day, at the same time. First Peter 1:3 says that when Christ was resurrected, we all were regenerated. (*The Intrinsic View of the Body of Christ*, p. 84)

Today's Reading

This great delivery, this great birth, of God's firstborn Son and His many brothers took place on the day of resurrection. But in another sense, in the process of time, this delivery has not been fully consummated. It is still going on in time. Whenever the local churches gain some increase, that is the continuation of that unique delivery. It will go on and on until the record in the heavens is fulfilled. This great, universal delivery will be fully consummated, completed, when the Lord comes back. (*The Intrinsic View of the Body of Christ*, p. 84)

Acts 13:33, quoting Psalm 2:7, indicates that Christ was begotten as the Son of God on the day of resurrection. In terms of His divinity, He did not need to be begotten to be the Son of God, but in terms of His humanity, He needed to be begotten....On the day of Christ's resurrection, His crucified humanity was enlivened by the

Spirit of His divinity and uplifted into the sonship of the only begotten Son of God. This is to be born through resurrection. Thus, in resurrection Christ was born as God's firstborn Son.

Christ's being the Firstborn implies that He has many brothers and that He is the Firstborn among the brothers. The birth through Christ's resurrection consisted not only of an individual birth but also of a corporate birth; this corporate entity includes God's firstborn Son and the believers as His many brothers....All of God's chosen people were born together with Christ in His resurrection. When Christ was resurrected, we were regenerated (1 Pet. 1:3). We were all born through this one universal delivery. (*Truth Lessons—Level Three*, vol. 3, p. 43)

The new child as the aggregate of all the children of God was brought forth in Christ's resurrection....When Christ was resurrected, we were regenerated to be children of God. The new child is the aggregate of all the children of God regenerated by God through the resurrection of Christ. Hence, the Lord's resurrection was a universal delivery, the delivery not of a single child but of a corporate child including Christ as the Head and His many brothers as the Body. This was the birth of a new corporate child comprising Christ and the believers.

The new child brought forth with Christ in His resurrection is the new man as the Body of Christ (Eph. 2:15; Col. 3:10-11). The birth of the new child was actually the birth of the new man. The old man was created by God in Genesis 1 and 2, but the new man was born through the resurrection of Christ. We were born into the old man, but we were regenerated into the new man. This new man includes Christ as the Head and all the believers as the Body. The Head is the firstborn Son of God, and the Body is a composition of all the many sons of God, the many brothers of the Lord. This new man, this child, was brought forth through Christ's death and resurrection. (*The Conclusion of the New Testament*, p. 1655)

Further Reading: The Conclusion of the New Testament, msg. 152; Crystallization-study of the Epistle to the Romans, msgs. 1, 3, 18

Enlightenment and inspiration:

WEEK 15 — DAY 6

Morning Nourishment

Psa. 87:7 Then singing as well as dancing, *they will say,* All my springs are in you.

John 4:14 But whoever drinks of the water that I will give him shall by no means thirst forever; but the water that I will give him will become in him a fountain of water springing up into eternal life.

Praise the Lord! In Zion we do not have mourning; we just have singing and dancing—all of them praising the Lord. In Zion we have many giants—David, Elijah, Peter, Paul, and others. But we also have many singing. We may not be the giants, but at least we are singing. You may think that you cannot sing well, but at least you can praise. All the singing and dancing are for praising. In Zion there are not many preachers and teachers, but there are many singing and dancing. They all say, "All my springs are in You" [Psa. 87:7]. The springs are the fountains of waters. All the springs and all the fountains are in the city of Zion. (*Christ and the Church Revealed and Typified in the Psalms,* p. 164)

Today's Reading

In the divine administration Christ is the Shepherd of the redeemed.... Under the shepherding of Christ, we shall not want (Psa. 23:1). Revelation 7:16 and 17 say, "They will not hunger anymore, neither will they thirst anymore, neither will the sun beat upon them, nor any heat; for the Lamb who is in the midst of the throne will shepherd them and guide them to springs of waters of life; and God will wipe away every tear from their eyes." Here we see that the Lamb will shepherd God's redeemed and guide them to springs of waters of life. As our Shepherd Christ will lead us into Himself as the spring of water of life so that we may enjoy the eternal dispensing of the Triune God. In eternity we shall drink of many springs and enjoy many different waters. (*The Conclusion of the New Testament,* p. 644).

The Triune God flows in the Divine Trinity in three stages....

When the fountain springs up, that is the fountain emerging. Then a river flows. The Father is the fountain, the Son is the spring, and the Spirit is the river.

This flowing Triune God is "into eternal life." The Greek preposition translated as *into* is rich in meaning. Here it speaks of the destination. The eternal life is the destination of the flowing Triune God. A fountain is in us springing up as a river into a destination. This destination is the eternal life. The New Jerusalem is the totality of the divine, eternal life. The eternal life eventually will be the New Jerusalem. Thus, *into eternal life* means *into the New Jerusalem*. We must have something flowing into that divine New Jerusalem in order for us to arrive there. The entire Bible is needed to interpret John 4:14. The Father is the fountain as the source, the Son is the spring, the Spirit is the flowing river, and this flowing issues in the eternal life, which is the New Jerusalem. The Gospel of John opens by saying, "In the beginning was the Word" (1:1). The Word is for speaking, and speaking is the start of God's flowing. Speaking is flowing, spreading is flowing, and dispensing is also flowing. God flows through speaking, through spreading, through dispensing.

We need to see that the Triune God is flowing through the Father, the Son, and the Spirit into us. When we drink of this water, it becomes a fountain in us. We all should say, "The fountain is in me!" This fountain emerges as a spring, and the spring flows out as a river for the New Jerusalem. This is the key to open up the entire Gospel of John. This is the divine speaking, divine spreading, divine dispensing, of the Divine Trinity. The Father as the fountain, the Son as the spring, and the Spirit as the river flow into us. When He flows into us, He flows with us. He will flow us into the New Jerusalem to be the New Jerusalem. (*Crystallization-study of the Gospel of John*, pp. 139, 141-142)

Further Reading: Crystallization-study of the Gospel of John, msgs. 3, 14; *Life-study of Isaiah,* msg. 40

Enlightenment and inspiration: _____

WEEK 15 — HYMN

Hymns, #1223

1. O walk about, walk about Zion,
   Go round about her in love.
   O walk about, walk about Zion
   And count the towers thereof.

2. O set your heart on her bulwarks,
   O set your heart on her walls,
   O set your heart on her bulwarks,
   Consider her palaces.

3. In elevation how beauteous,
   The joy of all the earth!
   In elevation how beauteous
   Is Zion, that city of worth!

4. O there is a river in Zion
   That flows so deep and so broad.
   O how the streams of that river
   Make glad the city of God!

5. Praise waiteth for Thee, Lord, in Zion,
   Praise waiteth, O God, for Thee,
   Praise waiteth for Thee, Lord, in Zion,
   For Zion is filled with Thee.

6. How great the Lord is in Zion,
   How greatly to be praised,
   How great He is in that city
   Which over the earth is raised.

7. O bless the Lord out of Zion,
   O let His praises swell,
   O bless the Lord out of Zion,
   Ye who in Jerusalem dwell.

8. The Lord bless thee out of Zion,
   The Lord bless thee o'er and o'er!
   The Lord bless thee out of Zion
   With life for evermore!

9. Behold how good and how pleasant
   With all the brethren to be!
   Behold how good and how pleasant
   To dwell in unity!

WEEK 15 — PROPHECY

10 O tell it to all generations,
    O tell it to all who will come,
    O tell it to all generations,
    The Spirit and Bride say, "Come!"

Composition for prophecy with main point and sub-points:

WEEK 16 — OUTLINE

The Highest and Fullest Experience of God—
Taking God as Our Habitation,
Our Eternal Dwelling Place

Scripture Reading: Psa. 90—92

Day 1 & Day 2

I. To take God as our habitation, our eternal dwelling place, is the highest and fullest experience of God (Psa. 90:1):
   A. Psalm 36:8 speaks of eating the fatness of God's house and drinking the river of God's pleasures, indicating that we can experience the Lord by eating and drinking Him (cf. John 6:48-58, 63; 7:37; 1 Cor. 10:3-4; 12:13).
   B. According to Moses, the giver of the law and the writer of Psalm 90, we can also dwell in the eternal Triune God as our Lord (v. 1; 91:9; Deut. 33:27; cf. John 15:4; 1 John 4:15-16; Rev. 21:22).
   C. To dwell in God is to have our living in God (Col. 2:6; 3:3; 1 John 4:16), taking Him as our everything; this is deeper than eating and drinking Him.
   D. Book Four of the Psalms (Psa. 90—106) unveils the saints' deeper experience of God in the identification with Christ, and it unveils God's recovery of His title and right over the earth:
      1. This indicates that our experience of dwelling in God paves the way for Christ to come to possess the earth so that God may recover His title (ownership) and right over the earth.
      2. Without the saints' deeper experience of God, God has no way to recover this title and right.

Day 3

   E. "The days of our years are seventy years, / Or, if because of strength, eighty years; / But their pride is labor and sorrow, / For it is soon gone, and we fly away" (90:10):
      1. If we take God as our dwelling place, we will realize that the span of our life on earth is brief and full of sins and afflictions (vv. 3-11).

2. We need to dwell in God, living in Him every minute, for outside of Him there are sins and afflictions (v. 8; John 16:33).
II. **Psalm 91 concerns the saints' identification with Christ in His taking God as His dwelling place (v. 9):**
   A. In their identification with Christ, the saints make Jehovah the Most High their habitation, dwelling in His secret place and abiding in His shadow under His wings (vv. 1-9).
   B. This is the genuine oneness with God; here, we are constituted with Him, and we and God live together as one.
   C. *You* and *Your* in verses 9 through 13 refer to Christ, as proven by the fact that verses 11 and 12 of this psalm are quoted by Satan in Matthew 4:6 in reference to Christ:
      1. This indicates that in Psalm 91 it is Christ who takes God as His habitation, His dwelling place.
      2. Thus, not only Moses took God as his dwelling place (90:1), but even the Lord Jesus, while He was on earth, took God the Father as His habitation.
      3. Moses, the lawgiver, and Christ, the grace-giver, were the same in taking God as their dwelling place, as their habitation.
      4. Thus, the saints (represented by Moses) and Christ are identified as one.
   D. To be identified with Christ is to be identified with Him not only in His death, in His resurrection, and in His ascension but also in His taking God as His habitation.
   E. If we would be identified with Christ in His death, resurrection, and ascension, we need to abide in Christ (John 15:4), and to abide in Christ is not only to remain in Him but also to dwell in Him, taking Him as our everything:
      1. We abide in Christ according to the teaching of the anointing inwardly and according to the walk of the Lord outwardly (1 John 2:27, 6).

2. In order to abide in Christ, we must keep God's commandments, God's charges to us, and be those who are submissive to God (3:24).
3. To abide in Christ, taking Him as our dwelling place, and to allow Him to abide in us, taking us as His dwelling place, are to live in the reality of the universal incorporation of the processed and consummated Triune God with the redeemed and regenerated believers (John 14:2, 10-11, 17, 20, 23):
   a. The New Jerusalem is the ultimate incorporation of the processed and consummated Triune God with the regenerated, sanctified, renewed, transformed, conformed, and glorified tripartite church (Rev. 21:3, 22).
   b. The New Jerusalem is the tabernacle of God, and the center of the tabernacle is Christ as the hidden manna; the way to be incorporated into this universal, divine-human incorporation, the mutual abode of God and man, is to eat Christ as the hidden manna (v. 3; Exo. 16:32-34; Heb. 9:4; Rev. 2:17).
4. We abide in Christ so that He may abide in us by dealing with the constant word in the Scriptures, which is outside of us, and the present word as the Spirit, which is within us (John 5:39-40; 6:63; 2 Cor. 3:6; Rev. 2:7):
   a. By the outward, written word we have the explanation, definition, and expression of the mysterious Lord, and by the inward, living word we have the experience of the abiding Christ and the presence of the practical Lord (Eph. 5:26; 6:17-18).
   b. If we abide in the Lord's constant and written word, His instant and living words will abide in us (John 8:31; 15:7; 1 John 2:14).
   c. We abide in Him and His words abide in us

so that we may speak in Him and He may speak in us for the building of God into man and of man into God (John 15:7; 2 Cor. 2:17; 13:3; 1 Cor. 14:4b).
  5. If we abide in Christ by loving Him, by always rejoicing, by unceasingly praying, and by giving thanks in everything, He will abide in us to dispense His riches into us (John 14:23; 1 Thes. 5:16-18; John 15:4).
  6. If we abide in Christ, we will bear much fruit to glorify God (v. 8).
  7. If we abide in Christ, when He is manifested, we will boldly meet Him and not be put to shame and depart from His glorious presence (1 John 2:28; cf. Matt. 25:30).
 F. *He, Him,* and *His* in Psalm 91:14-16 refer to Christ; these verses are a prophecy concerning Christ:
  1. Christ loved God the Father (John 14:31); He has been set on high, exalted to the highest place in the heavens (Phil. 2:9-11); and He is now seeing God's salvation in the extension of His days in resurrection (Psa. 91:16; Rev. 1:18a).
  2. In all these matters we should be identified with Christ; then we will live with Him and love God; thus, we will be exalted, and we will see God's salvation in the extension of our days.

Day 6 III. **Psalm 92 shows the issue of the deeper experience of God in the saints' identification with Christ in taking God as their dwelling place:**
 A. The first issue is that the saints rejoice in the great works of Jehovah (vv. 1-9); when we dwell in God, taking Him as our habitation, we see His great works in the accomplishing of His economy and rejoice in them.
 B. Before we dwell in God as our habitation, we may be low and frequently defeated; a further issue of our dwelling in God is that our horn (fighting strength) is exalted over our spiritual enemies (v. 10; Eph. 6:10-13).

WEEK 16 — OUTLINE

C. Another issue of our dwelling in God as our habitation is our being mingled with fresh oil, which signifies the consummated Spirit, who is fresh and present (cf. Exo. 30:23-25).

D. Still another issue of our dwelling in God, taking Him as everything in our living in His house, is that we are securely planted in His house and flourish in the riches of His divine life to such an extent that we bear fruit even in old age (Psa. 92:12-14).

WEEK 16 — DAY 1

Morning Nourishment

Psa. 90:1 O Lord, You have been our dwelling place in all generations.

17 And let the favor of the Lord our God be upon us, and establish the work of our hands upon us; indeed the work of our hands, establish it.

John 15:4 Abide in Me and I in you. As the branch cannot bear fruit of itself unless it abides in the vine, so neither *can* you unless you abide in Me.

We will consider Psalms 90 through 92. As we read these psalms, we need to seek what they reveal about the deeper experience of God and about the identification with Christ.

Psalm 90 opens with a word concerning God as our dwelling place....To be sure, the Bible is the only book that tells us that God can be our dwelling place. Psalm 42:1 speaks of panting after God as a hart pants after streams of water. In preaching the gospel, we may tell others that they can drink, eat, and breathe the Lord Jesus, but have you ever told others that they can dwell in the Lord? Dwelling in the Lord is deeper than drinking Him. Many of us, after coming into the church life, can testify of drinking, eating, and breathing Christ, but have you ever had the thought of dwelling in Christ? (*Life-study of the Psalms,* p. 398)

Today's Reading

Psalms is not a book on good and evil...[but] a book on drinking Christ, eating Christ, breathing Christ, and dwelling in Christ. Christ is the living water to quench our thirst. In Psalm 36 the river of God's pleasures is for our drinking, and the fatness of God's house is for our eating. We can drink, eat, and breathe the Lord. Now in Psalm 90 we see that we can also dwell in the Lord.

Psalm 90 was written by Moses, the one who gave the law with all the statutes and ordinances. In verse 1 this lawgiver, who was quite old, proclaimed that God is our dwelling place in all generations. Then in verse 2 he went on to say, "Before the mountains were brought forth, / And before You gave birth to the earth and the world, / Indeed from eternity to eternity, You are God." This was a new thought, something altogether unprecedented. Have you ever considered this matter of God's being our dwelling place? From my youth I was taught by Bible teachers regarding the abiding in Christ mentioned in John 15....At that time I understood the word "abide" as meaning to stay or to remain, not to dwell. But eventually I learned that the Greek word translated "abide" means not simply to remain but also to dwell. To abide in Christ is to dwell in Him, not just remain or stay in Him. When we dwell in our house, we have our life and our living there.... Furthermore, our house indicates the kind of person we are.

According to Moses' word in Psalm 90:1, our house, our dwelling place, is the Triune God as our Lord....When we experience the Triune God to the degree that we take Him as our dwelling place, we have the deeper experience of God. (*Life-study of the Psalms*, pp. 398-399)

Psalm 90 begins with the Lord as our dwelling place and ends with the favor of the Lord. This is certainly not the teaching of the law. Psalm 90 tells us that the eternal God is our habitation. We may find in God our everlasting home. A thousand years to Him are like yesterday when it passes by and like a watch in the night—a mere two or three hours (v. 4). Such a God is our dwelling place. We may dwell in Him; we may abide under His covering, and thus His favor will be upon us. It is not a matter of keeping the law, but of taking God as our dwelling place. It is a matter of putting the eternal God upon us as our favor.

[Verse 17 says,] "Let the favor of the Lord our God be upon us, / And establish the work of our hands upon us." If we are in such a position, we are those who are really working for God, and our work will be established by His hands. It is not keeping the Ten Commandments but dwelling in God and letting His favor be upon us. Only thus are we qualified to do His work, and only thus will our work be established by His hands. This is Psalm 90. (*Christ and the Church Revealed and Typified in the Psalms*, pp. 170-171)

Further Reading: A Living of Mutual Abiding with the Lord in Spirit, ch. 3

Enlightenment and inspiration: ___

WEEK 16 — DAY 2

Morning Nourishment

Psa. For You have made Jehovah, *who is* my refuge,
91:9 *even* the Most High, Your habitation.
11-12 For He will give His angels charge concerning You to keep You in all Your ways. They will bear You up in their hands, lest You dash Your foot against a stone.

As we have indicated, Psalms 90 through 92 are about the saints' deeper experience of God in the identification with Christ. We have seen that the deeper experience of God is to dwell in God, but what is revealed in these psalms concerning the identification with Christ? To answer this question we need to read 91:9: "You have made Jehovah, who is my refuge,/Even the Most High, Your habitation." Moses, the writer of Psalm 90, took Jehovah as his dwelling place, and the writer of Psalm 91 did the same thing. Verses 11 and 12 indicate that "You" and "Your" in verse 9 refer to Christ. These verses are quoted in Matthew 4:6 and applied to Christ. This reveals that not only Moses took God as his dwelling place, but even the Lord Jesus, while He was on earth, took God the Father as His habitation. Moses, the lawgiver, and Christ, the grace-giver, were the same in taking God as their dwelling place, as their habitation. (*Life-study of the Psalms,* pp. 399-400)

Today's Reading

To take God as our habitation, our dwelling place, is the highest and fullest experience of God. To take God as our dwelling place is to experience Him to the fullest extent. Probably no one among us would dare to say that he dwells in God all the time. But this is what Christ did. When He was living His human life on earth, He continually took God the Father as His habitation.

To be identified with Christ is to be identified with Him not only in His death, in His resurrection, and in His ascension but also in His taking God as His habitation. We are identified with Christ to such an extent. A number of good books have been written on our identification with Christ in His death, resurrection, and ascension. Jessie Penn-Lewis emphasized the identification with Christ in His death; T. Austin-Sparks, the identification with Christ in His resurrection; and Brother Nee, the identification with Christ in His ascension. If we would be identified with Christ in His death, resurrection, and ascension, we need to abide in Christ. If we do not abide in Christ, we are separated from Him and thus are not identified with Him. The only way that we can be identified with Christ in His death, resurrection, and ascension is to abide in Christ, and to abide in Christ is not only to remain in Him but also to dwell in Him, taking Him as our everything.

To dwell in our house means that we have our living there in many different ways. For instance, I eat my meals at home, sitting in my comfortable seat at the dining table. Likewise, to dwell in God is to have our living in God. Often we speak about eating Christ, but we need to see that when we eat Christ, we should be dwelling in Him.

Psalms Book 4 unveils the saints' deeper experience of God in the identification with Christ and God's recovery of His title and right over the earth. This indicates that our experience of dwelling in God paves the way for Christ to come to possess the earth that God may recover His title and right over the earth. *Title* refers to ownership, and *right* refers to all God's rights over the earth. Without the saints' deeper experience of God, God has no way to recover this title and right. This means that if we drink Christ, eat Christ, and breathe Christ without taking Christ as our habitation, God has no way to recover the earth.

This thought is found in John 15. In John 14:2 the Lord Jesus said, "In My Father's house are many abodes;...I go to prepare a place for you." These abodes are not rooms in a heavenly mansion, as commonly supposed, but places in the Father's house. In 15:4 the Lord went on to say, "Abide in Me." This reveals that Christ is not only the way to the house—He is the house itself. To abide in Christ is to dwell in Him. By our dwelling in Him Christ has a way to recover the earth. (*Life-study of the Psalms*, pp. 400-401)

Further Reading: Life-study of the Psalms, msg. 35

Enlightenment and inspiration:

WEEK 16 — DAY 3

Morning Nourishment

Psa. 90:8-10 You have set our iniquities before You, our secret *sins* in the light of Your countenance....We bring our years to an end like a sigh. The days of our years are seventy years, or, if because of strength, eighty years; but their pride is labor and sorrow, for it is soon gone, and we fly away.

12 Teach us then to number our days that we may gain a heart of wisdom.

If you take God as your dwelling place, you will realize that the span of your life on earth is short (Psa. 90:3-11). In verse 10 Moses said, "The days of our years are seventy years, / Or, if because of strength, eighty years...." With the Lord, however, a thousand years are "like yesterday when it passes by / And like a watch in the night" (v. 4). According to the Bible, the person who lived the longest was Methuselah; he lived nine hundred sixty-nine years. In the sight of God, however, this was less than a day. The short span of our life is full of sins and afflictions. If one has such a realization, he must be one who takes God as his dwelling place. I want to dwell in God, living in Him every minute, for outside of Him there are sins and afflictions. (*Life-study of the Psalms*, p. 402)

Today's Reading

Moses, writing according to the realization that comes from dwelling in God, prayed, "Teach us then to number our days / That we may gain a heart of wisdom" (Psa. 90:12). Gaining a heart of wisdom enables us to live a glad and rejoicing life (vv. 13-17). Moses had the deep feeling that he needed to learn how to number his days so that he could live a happy life. As we look back upon yesterday, we may feel shameful. This indicates that we need to let God teach us how to number our days. Young people may not understand the meaning of this, but as an elderly person I can testify that I do know how to number my days. I number every day.

The matter of the identification with Christ is unveiled in Psalm 91....In the identification with Christ, the saints make

Jehovah the Most High their habitation, dwelling in His secret place and abiding in His shadow under His wings (vv. 1-9). We all need to dwell in God by dwelling in the secret place (v. 1). This is the real oneness with God. Here God becomes us; we are constituted with Him; and we and God live together as one.

In the identification with Christ, we are under the keeping care of the angels, and we tread upon the enemy Satan (vv. 11-13; Matt. 4:6). Psalm 91:13 says, "You will tread upon the lion and the cobra; / You will trample the young lion and the serpent." Here Satan is likened to a lion that devours God's people and to a serpent that poisons God's people. In Matthew 4 we see that while the Lord Jesus was living a human life on earth, He was under the care of the angels, who protected Him from Satan and the evil spirits. Matthew 4:11 says that angels came and ministered to Him. The angels are also protecting and safeguarding us today, as indicated by Hebrews 1.

In the identification with Christ, the saints set their love upon God; they are set on high by Him; and they see His salvation in the extension of their days (Psa. 91:14-16). These verses are a prophecy referring to Christ. Christ set His love upon God the Father. Christ has been exalted to the highest place in the heavens, and He is now seeing God's salvation in the extension of His days in resurrection. Christ died, but in resurrection He will live forever. Therefore, He could say, "I became dead, and behold, I am living forever and ever" (Rev. 1:18a). This is the extension of His days in resurrection for the carrying out of His salvation prophesied not only in Psalm 91 but also in Isaiah 53.

If we are identified with Christ, we too will take God as our habitation. We will be one with Christ in His crucifixion, in His resurrection, in His ascension, and in His taking God as His habitation. Then we will live with Him and set our love upon God. Thus, we will be exalted, and we will see God's salvation in the extension of our days. (*Life-study of the Psalms*, pp. 402-404)

Further Reading: *Life-study of the Psalms*, msg. 35

Enlightenment and inspiration: _____

Morning Nourishment

1 John 2:27 And as for you, the anointing which you have received from Him abides in you, and you have no need that anyone teach you; but as His anointing teaches you concerning all things and is true and is not a lie, and even as it has taught you, abide in Him.

6 He who says he abides in Him ought himself also to walk even as He walked.

3:24 And he who keeps His commandments abides in Him, and He in him....

To abide in Christ, on the one hand, we must be according to the teaching of the anointing of the Holy Spirit inwardly, and on the other hand, we must walk as the Lord walked outwardly [1 John 2:27, 6]. This means that we must abide in Christ according to the teaching of the Holy Spirit inwardly and according to the walk of the Lord outwardly....To abide in Christ...we must keep God's commandments, God's charges to us, and be those who are submissive to God [1 John 3:24]. (*Life Lessons*, vol. 3, pp. 24-25)

Today's Reading

The way to abide is by the anointing. All believers have the Spirit within them, and this Spirit is not silent, passive, or inactive. He is very active and aggressive and is constantly moving and working within us....If there is nothing or no one living within us, there will be no moving or working within us. However, every saved person has received the Holy Spirit (Rom. 8:9, 11).

The word *teaches* [in 1 John 2:27] indicates that the moving of the compound Spirit is full of meaning. However, we need the proper knowledge of the Bible to understand the meaning of the Spirit's moving. For this reason, we all need to read the Bible to accumulate the necessary knowledge. (*Crucial Principles for the Christian Life and the Church Life*, pp. 32, 37-38)

The way to be incorporated into the tabernacle is to eat the hidden manna. The more we eat Christ, the more we are incorporated into the Triune God as a universal incorporation.... The tabernacle in the Old Testament was a figure of the New

Jerusalem, which is called the tabernacle of God. As the tabernacle of God the New Jerusalem is the universal incorporation. This universal incorporation is God's eternal goal. The New Jerusalem is the tabernacle of God, and the center of this tabernacle is Christ as the hidden manna for us to eat. The way to be in the New Jerusalem is to eat Christ.

I began to love the Bible from the day I was saved in 1925. I have spent the past seventy-one years studying the Bible, but it was not until recently that I saw so clearly that the goal of God's economy is the enlarged, universal, divine-human incorporation of the consummated God with the regenerated believers. The unbelievers will go into the lake of fire. They have nothing to do with this universal incorporation. But all of the believers will eventually be incorporated into this one great incorporation. The final consummation of this universal incorporation is the New Jerusalem. Mainly three apostles—Paul, Peter, and John—present this revelation to us in their Epistles piece by piece and bit by bit. By the Lord's mercy, we have put these pieces together to see a full and complete vision of this universal incorporation. (*The Issue of Christ Being Glorified by the Father with the Divine Glory*, pp. 31, 44)

The first issue of our abiding in Christ is that Christ and God abide in us to dispense Their riches to us, supplying and transfusing them into us [John 15:4; 1 John 3:24]....If we abide in Christ, He also will abide in us, enabling us to enjoy all the riches of His life. Thus, we will bear much fruit to glorify God, that is to live out God that He may be expressed in us [John 15:5, 8]....If we abide in Christ and bear much fruit by His life to glorify God, when He is manifested, we will boldly meet Him and not be put to shame from His glorious presence ([1 John 2:28]; cf. Matt. 25:30). (*Life Lessons*, vol. 3, p. 25)

Further Reading: Life Lessons, vol. 3, lsn. 27; *Crucial Principles for the Christian Life and the Church Life*, ch. 3; *The Issue of Christ Being Glorified by the Father with the Divine Glory*, chs. 4-5

Enlightenment and inspiration: _____

WEEK 16 — DAY 5

Morning Nourishment

1 Thes. 5:16-18 Always rejoice, unceasingly pray, in everything give thanks; for this is the will of God in Christ Jesus for you.

John 15:7 If you abide in Me and My words abide in you, ask whatever you will, and it shall be done for you.

The Triune God...enters into us to abide in our spirit with all that He has, all that He has gone through, all that He has accomplished, and all that He is....Therefore, every day from morning to evening, in big things or in small things, in our home or outside our home, and in all our living and actions we must abide in Him. When we want to speak to others, unless we have the assurance that we are abiding in Him, we should not speak.

When you abide in Him, you are soaked with Him. When you abide in Him, you give Him the condition to abide in you. Thus, you will enjoy all His riches. (*A Living of Mutual Abiding with the Lord in Spirit*, pp. 45, 47)

Today's Reading

According to our experience, if we pray and also give thanks, even if before we were not abiding in the Lord, we will spontaneously enter into the Lord and abide in Him. If we want to get in and not come out but remain inside all the time, we need to pray unceasingly and give thanks in everything.

A vile sinner needs only to believe and repent, praying to the Lord, "Lord Jesus, I am truly a vile sinner. I pray that You save me." Immediately the "connection" is made, and Christ enters into him. This sinner, however, still has to say, "Lord Jesus, I really thank You." Then the light in him will shine, and he will abide in the Lord. Hence, whether we are believers or sinners, we all need to abide in the Lord through prayer and thanksgiving.

Among the twenty-seven books of the New Testament, only three—1 Thessalonians, Colossians, and Ephesians—

mention the matter of giving thanks in everything. All three of these books were written by the apostle Paul, and their contents show a sequence that is mysterious and wonderful. The first of these books, 1 Thessalonians, speaks of how we can be saved and how we should have a holy life so that our spirit, soul, and body may be wholly sanctified, making us ready to meet the Lord at His coming. This concerns a proper, general Christian life. The second book is Colossians, which concerns Christ and which eventually speaks about experiencing Christ. The life of experiencing Christ is a life of giving thanks in everything. Not only is the proper, general Christian life a life of giving thanks in everything, but also the life of experiencing Christ is ultimately a matter of giving thanks for all things. The third book, Ephesians, which is a sister book to Colossians, concerns the church, and at the end it speaks about the experience of the church. We can have the church life only by living in the spirit. Likewise, such a church life is a matter of giving thanks in all things.

What does it mean to "unceasingly pray"? We must understand and realize that we have a spirit within us, which is our spiritual breathing organ. The reason we do not want to pray or cannot pray is that we basically do not use our spirit. To pray, we must use our spirit. Whenever we use our spirit, we are enlivened. The first function of our spirit is to pray. Your spirit prays automatically even without your prompting. Hence, in order to pray unceasingly, you must not interrupt your spirit's activity. Instead, you must allow your spirit to be active all the time.

When we live and walk in our activated spirit, we pray unceasingly, and spontaneously we abide in the Lord and enjoy Him as our life. (*Abiding in the Lord to Enjoy His Life*, pp. 31-32, 36, 38)

Further Reading: Abiding in the Lord to Enjoy His Life, chs. 1-3; *The Mending Ministry of John*, ch. 8

Enlightenment and inspiration: _____

Morning Nourishment

Psa. But You have exalted my horn like that of a wild
92:10 ox; I am anointed with fresh oil.
12-14 The righteous man will flourish like the palm tree; he will grow like a cedar in Lebanon. Planted in the house of Jehovah, they will flourish in the courts of our God. They will still bring forth fruit in old age; they will be full of sap and green.

Psalm 92 shows us the issue of the deeper experience of God in the identification with Christ....First, the issue is that the saints rejoice in the great works of Jehovah (vv. 1-9). If we do not dwell in God, not taking God as our habitation, we may see many things, but these things will be insignificant. But when we dwell in God, taking Him as our habitation, we see His great works...and rejoice in them.

The Hebrew word translated "anointed" [in verse 10] (the same word used in Leviticus 2:4) can also be rendered "mingled." The fresh oil is the consummated Spirit, who is fresh and present. I can testify that in the last five years I have enjoyed being mingled with fresh oil more than ever, and I have been full of joy in the Lord. (*Life-study of the Psalms,* p. 404)

Today's Reading

The poetry [in Psalm 92:12-14] is a picture of those who experience God in a deeper way by dwelling in Him, taking Him as everything in their living in the house of God. (*Life-study of the Psalms*, p. 405)

Psalm 92 shows the results of taking God as our dwelling place. When we and the Lord Jesus take God as our home, the issue first is that we will sing praises. "It is good to give thanks to Jehovah / And to sing psalms to Your name, O Most High" (v. 1). Only by dwelling in God, by taking God as our habitation, and by letting His favor be upon us, can we be filled with His praises. This is the first result. The second result is indicated in verse 4: "You have made me rejoice, O Jehovah, because of what You have done; / Because of the works of Your hands I will shout for joy." We must put Psalm 90:17 together with this verse: "Establish the work of our hands upon us; / Indeed the work of our hands, establish it." By combining these two portions, we see that to dwell in God as our habitation causes us to realize what the work of God is. Continuing in Psalm 92, we read, "How great are Your works, O Jehovah!" (v. 5)....The great work of God is to restore the desolated building of God and to recover the sons of Korah. The great work of God today is first to recover the local churches and second to recover so many of you. Many of us are the real sons of Korah. God's great work is to recover the things desolated by Satan. Only by dwelling in His house can we realize this work in all its greatness.

In God's house, dwelling in God as our habitation, we have a daily sense of such a mingling with fresh oil [v. 10]. Do you have this kind of feeling? Day by day I sense something so fresh, not just as water but as oil, being mingled with me....[I am fresh] because I am being daily mingled with fresh oil.

When God is our habitation in the local churches, we are like palms and cedars, so stately and secure, planted in the house of God [vv. 12-13]....If we are planted, we are bound; it is not easy for us to move. But it is here that we flourish....We flourish to such an extent that even when we are old, we still bring forth fruit; we are full of sap and green [v. 14]. Only by taking God and the local church as our habitation can we do this. God and the local church as our habitation are not two separate things, but one. If we are truly dwelling in the local church, we are certainly dwelling in God; and if we are one with God, surely we are dwelling in the local church. Then we are planted in the divine habitation, flourishing in the courts of our God, and bringing forth fruit even in old age, full of song and praise. The longer we dwell here, the younger we become. (*Christ and the Church Revealed and Typified in the Psalms*, pp. 171-173)

Further Reading: Christ and the Church Revealed and Typified in the Psalms, ch. 16

Enlightenment and inspiration: _____
_____
_____
_____

WEEK 16 — HYMN

Hymns, #564

1. I have learned the wondrous secret
   Of abiding in the Lord;
   I have tasted life's pure fountain,
   I am drinking of His word;
   I have found the strength and sweetness
   Of abiding 'neath the blood;
   I have lost myself in Jesus,
   I am sinking into God.

   I'm abiding in the Lord
   And confiding in His word;
   I am hiding in the bosom of His love.
   Yes, abiding in the Lord
   And confiding in His word,
   I am hiding in the bosom of His love.

2. I am crucified with Jesus,
   And He lives and dwells with me;
   I have ceased from all my struggling,
   'Tis no longer I, but He.
   All my will is yielding to Him,
   And His Spirit reigns within;
   And His precious blood each moment
   Keeps me cleansed and free from sin.

3. All my sicknesses I bring Him,
   And He bears them all away;
   All my fears and griefs I tell Him,
   All my cares from day to day,
   All my strength I draw from Jesus,
   By His breath I live and move;
   E'en His very mind He gives me,
   And His faith, and life, and love.

4. For my words I take His wisdom,
   For my works His Spirit's power;
   For my ways His ceaseless presence
   Guards and guides me every hour.
   Of my heart, He is the portion,
   Of my joy the boundless spring;
   Savior, Sanctifier, Healer,
   Glorious Lord, and coming King.

WEEK 16 — PROPHECY

Composition for prophecy with main point and sub-points:

WEEK 17 — OUTLINE

Christ's Eternal and Unchanging Existence in His Resurrection

Scripture Reading: Psa. 102:6-8, 13, 16, 21-28

Day 1

I. Psalm 102 unveils Christ's death and His eternal and unchanging existence in His resurrection:
   A. In typology, this psalm first refers to Christ's suffering, especially to His death:
      1. Christ's suffering was for redemption, and His redemption was to produce the church as the house of God and the city of God (vv. 6-8).
      2. Verse 7 is a particular verse concerning Christ's suffering, which was related to His zeal for God's house (John 2:17; Psa. 69:9):
         a. In Psalm 102:7 Christ is likened to a lone sparrow on a housetop, referring to the flat roof of a Jewish house, where people would often go to pray (Acts 10:9).
         b. This indicates that when the Lord Jesus was on earth, probably there were times when in the night He, like a lone bird on a housetop, would watch and pray, caring not for His own interest but for the interest of God and of God's house (Matt. 14:23; Luke 6:12).

Day 2

   B. Psalm 102:23-28 unveils Christ as the One who is everlasting in His resurrection:
      1. Verses 25 through 27, quoted in Hebrews 1:10-12, speak of Christ's continuing existence in His resurrection.
      2. Christ's existence is unchanging throughout all generations because of His resurrection (Acts 2:24; Rev. 1:18; Heb. 13:8).
      3. The resurrected Christ is no longer bound by any limitations; when He resurrected, nothing could hold Him back (John 20:1-18; Acts 2:24):

WEEK 17 — OUTLINE

   a. Resurrection means that the Lord Jesus has broken through all barriers, even the greatest barrier of all—death; death has been nullified, and the resurrected Christ lives forever and ever (Heb. 2:14; 2 Tim. 1:10; Rev. 1:18).
   b. In His resurrection Christ has transcended everything, including space and time; as the resurrected One, He is omnipresent, and space and time cannot limit Him (Eph. 1:19-23).
  4. Because of His eternal and unchanging existence in His resurrection, Christ is the key that turns the earth to the Lord (Psa. 102:12-27; Rev. 1:18; Heb. 13:8).

Day 3
II. **The product of Christ's death and resurrection is the church, typified by Zion with God's house and God's city** (Psa. 102:13-16, 21; Heb. 12:22-23):
 A. In Psalm 102 Zion, the center of the city of Jerusalem, typifies the church as the center of God's kingdom (48:2; Matt. 16:18-19).
 B. The stones typify the believers as the building materials of the church, and the dust, the soil, typifies the ground of the church (Psa. 102:14; 1 Pet. 2:5; Rev. 1:11):
  1. We should take pleasure in all the members of the church (Psa. 102:14).
  2. We should favor the ground of the church, which is the ground of oneness (Deut. 12:5-28; 14:23-25; John 17:11, 21-23; 1 Cor. 1:10-13a; Eph. 4:3-6; Rev. 1:11).
 C. In Psalm 102:16 the rebuilding of Zion typifies the rebuilding of the church:
  1. It is through the established, restored Zion, signifying the church, that all the nations and kingdoms will be brought into the praise and worship of Jehovah (vv. 21-22).
  2. The rebuilding of the devastated church, typified by the rebuilding of Zion, will turn

WEEK 17 — OUTLINE

all the nations to the Lord, and the kingdom of the world will become the kingdom of God and of Christ (v. 16; Rev. 11:15).

Day 4

III. It is in Christ's resurrection, by Christ's resurrection, and through Christ's resurrection that the church continues its existence (Psa. 102:21-28; Matt. 16:18; Eph. 1:19-23; 2:6):

A. Christ's resurrection enables the church to continue its existence (Matt. 16:18; Acts 1:22; 2:31; 4:2, 33).

B. The church, the Body of Christ, is absolutely in resurrection (Matt. 16:18; Eph. 1:19-23; 2:6):

 1. The golden lampstand, typifying the church as the Body of Christ, portrays Christ as the resurrection life, growing, branching, budding, and blossoming to shine the light (Exo. 25:31-40; Num. 17:8; Rev. 1:11-12).

 2. The church is a new creation in Christ's resurrection and was created by the resurrected Christ (Gal. 6:15; Heb. 2:10-12):

 a. We are the Body of Christ only in the new creation germinated by Christ's resurrection life (2 Cor. 5:17; Eph. 1:19-23).

 b. The reality of resurrection is Christ as the life-giving Spirit (John 11:25; 20:22; 1 Cor. 15:45b):

 1) If we do any work that is not in resurrection, the life-giving Spirit will not honor it.

 2) The Spirit honors only what is in resurrection (vv. 45b, 58).

Day 5

 3. In order to be in the reality of the Body of Christ, we need to be absolutely in the resurrection life of Christ (John 11:25; 1 Cor. 15:45b; 2 Cor. 1:9):

 a. When we do not live by our natural life but live by the divine life within us, we are in resurrection; the issue of this is the Body of Christ (Phil. 3:10-11; 2 Cor. 1:9).

WEEK 17 — OUTLINE

b. Our natural strength and ability need to be dealt with by the cross to become useful in resurrection for our service to the Lord (Phil. 3:3).

C. The church is "resurrectionly"; that is, the church is an organic entity absolutely in resurrection, a new creation created in Christ's resurrection and by the resurrected Christ (Eph. 1:19-23; 2:6; 2 Cor. 5:17):

1. "God sees the church as a being that can endure death. The gates of Hades are open to the church, but the gates of Hades cannot prevail against her and cannot confine her; thus, the nature of the church is resurrection" (*The Orthodoxy of the Church*, pp. 21-22).

Day 6

2. The church is the vessel that holds the resurrected Christ; the church is the place where God demonstrates the operation of the might of His strength, according to the power which He caused to operate in Christ when He raised Him from the dead (Eph. 1:19-23; 2:6).

3. The church is the same as the resurrected Lord not only in nature but also in power (John 11:25; Matt. 16:18; Acts 4:33; Rev. 1:11, 18; 2:8).

4. Just as God broke through all barriers in the resurrected Christ, He is breaking through all barriers in the church; therefore, the church should be the same in life and power as the resurrected Christ (Eph. 1:19-23; 2:6):

a. The church should be as powerful, as free, and as unfettered by any limitation as the Lord Jesus is (Rev. 1:18).

b. The might of God's strength not only operated in Christ, but it continually operates in the church as well (Eph. 1:19-20; Col. 1:29).

c. The power of the church is the resurrection power of Christ (Phil. 3:10).

5. The Holy Spirit is manifesting the resurrection power of Christ through the church (Acts 1:8; 2:24; 4:33):

WEEK 17 — OUTLINE

   a. The church is the depository and storehouse of the resurrection power of Christ (Eph. 1:19-23).
   b. Hades represents death, and the church represents resurrection (Matt. 16:18).
   c. As Christ is in resurrection, the church also is in resurrection; therefore, the church continues its existence in the resurrection of Christ (Eph. 1:19-23; 2:6; Rev. 1:18, 20).

WEEK 17 — DAY 1

Morning Nourishment

Luke 6:12 And in these days He went out to the mountain to pray, and He spent the whole night in prayer to God.

Psa. 102:7 I watch, and I am like a lone sparrow on a housetop.

We may say that the Psalms are an extract of the entire Bible. The Bible begins with God's existence and then goes on to speak of God's creation, which has certain indications concerning Christ. Out of Christ there issues the church, which is God's house. When the church as God's house is strengthened and enlarged, it becomes the city, that is, the kingdom of God. Eventually, the kingdom of God will bring in the restoration of the earth during the millennium, which will consummate in the new heaven and the new earth with the New Jerusalem—the consummation of God's house and God's kingdom—as the center. This extract of the Bible in the Psalms is a key that opens the whole Bible. (*Life-study of the Psalms*, p. 415)

Today's Reading

We come to another group of psalms consisting of Psalms 102 through 106, which is somewhat hard to understand. In this group we first see Christ. Psalm 102 is a psalm on Christ. Strong evidence of this is the quotation of verses 25 through 27 in Hebrews 1:10-12.

The title of Psalm 102 tells us that it is a prayer of an afflicted one, one who was suffering. The psalmist, a godly one, was suffering because of the destruction and devastation of Zion with the temple and the holy city. He suffered to such an extent that he was fainting. In this matter he was somewhat like Jeremiah who, after the destruction of Jerusalem and the temple, sat on a mountain outside the city, looked at the devastation of the temple and the city, and wrote the book of Lamentations, probably fainting as he did so. The godly one who wrote Psalm 102 was also afflicted by the destruction of the temple and the city. Fainting because of his suffering, he prayed to God and poured out his complaint. The word "complaint" in the title of this psalm does not mean that the psalmist was complaining to God; rather, here this word denotes a miserable situation—the suffering caused by the destruction of the temple and the city of Jerusalem.

In typology, Psalm 102 first refers to Christ's suffering, especially to His death. Christ's suffering consummated in His death, and through His death the church, God's house, came into existence. Eventually, the church as God's house becomes God's city, God's kingdom. Ephesians 2:19, therefore, refers both to the household of God and to the kingdom of God.

Christ's being the key that turns the earth to the Lord is based upon His suffering (Psa. 102: 6-8). The "housetop" [in verse 7] refers to the flat roof of a Jewish house. People would often go to the housetop to pray. Peter did this in Acts 10:9. Since Psalm 102:7 refers to Christ, this verse indicates that when the Lord Jesus was on earth, probably there were times when in the night He, like a lone sparrow on a housetop, would watch and pray, caring for God's interest. This was also the situation of the writer of this psalm. Because of the devastation of Zion, he could not sleep nor stay in bed. Instead, he went to the housetop where he poured out his complaint to God, asking Him to look upon Zion, the city, and the temple.

Psalm 102:7 is a particular verse concerning Christ's suffering, His affliction. His affliction was related to His zeal for God's house (John 2:17; Psa. 69:9). In His suffering Christ was a watcher, caring not for His own interest but for the interest of God's house. Thus, He likened Himself to a lone sparrow on the roof of a house. As He was watching for God's interest, He was like a lone sparrow on a housetop. This was an aspect of Christ's suffering.

As we have pointed out, Christ's suffering was for the producing of the church. Today's Christians realize that Christ's suffering, which consummated in His death, was for redemption, but very few realize that His suffering was also for the producing of the church. We need to see that Christ's death was for redemption to produce the church. (*Life-study of the Psalms*, pp. 416-417, 419)

Further Reading: Life-study of the Psalms, msg. 37; Christ and the Church Revealed and Typified in the Psalms, ch. 18

Enlightenment and inspiration: _____

_____
_____
_____

WEEK 17 — DAY 2

Morning Nourishment

Psa. Of old You laid the foundation of the earth, and the
102:25 heavens are the work of Your hands.
27-28 But You are the same, and Your years are without end. The children of Your servants will continue, and their seed will be established before You.

Psalm 102 has three sections. Verses 1 through 11 are the first section, concerned with suffering and affliction; verses 12 through 22 are the second section, concerned with the rebuilding of Zion, the restoration of the destroyed temple and holy city; and verses 23 through 28 are the third section, unveiling the Lord as the One who is everlasting in His resurrection....Resurrection is the lengthening of the Lord's days; He will exist forever and ever in His resurrection. (*Life-study of the Psalms,* p. 416)

Today's Reading

[Psalm 102:25-27], quoted in Heb. 1:10-12, speaks of Christ's continuing existence in His resurrection. Christ is the key that turns the earth to the Lord because of His eternal and unchanging existence (Rev. 1:18; Heb. 13:8). Christ's suffering (Psa. 102:6-8) was for redemption, and His redemption was to produce the church as the house of God and the city of God (John 19:34 and footnote). It is in Christ's resurrection, by Christ's resurrection, and through Christ's resurrection that the church continues its existence and will consummate in the restoration (Psa. 102:12-22; Matt. 19:28; Acts 3:21), in which the entire earth with the peoples of all the nations will turn to the Lord (Psa. 102:21-22; Isa. 2:2-3; Zech. 8:20-22). (Psa. 102:25, footnote 1)

Only He who passed through resurrection can fulfill God's plan. Hebrews 1:5 says, "You are My Son; this day have I begotten You." This word refers to the Lord's ascent from the grave. After His resurrection, the Lord rose from the grave, and God said to Him, "This day have I begotten You." When God said, "This day have I begotten You," He had found the man He was after.

Since His birth at Bethlehem, the Lord was a moral man.

WEEK 17 — DAY 2

But after His resurrection, He was manifested to be a man of power. After His resurrection, He became omnipresent. Time and space could limit Him no longer. He became a man endowed with resurrection power. He is now the man God wants, and God's plan of creating man is fulfilled.

After the Lord resurrected, time and space were no longer constraints to Him. Death could not contain Him. Through His resurrection He broke the barrier of death. Lazarus's resurrection...was only a kind of resuscitation to life; it was not actually a resurrection. Lazarus was not able to break even the bondage of his grave clothes. In the end he still had to go through death. The limitation of death still remained with him. When the Lord resurrected, however, He broke the barrier of death. He passed through death but was not held by death (Acts 2:24). The gates of Hades could not stop Him; they could not swallow Him. He resurrected, and He will die no more. Death has no power or leverage over Him....When Mary the Magdalene went and told Peter and John about the Lord's disappearance from the grave, the two disciples went to look for Him. They only found the linen cloths and the handkerchief which had been over His head folded up in one place; however, the Lord was not there (John 20:1-8). It was like a man who had put on his coat and buttoned it, but who had disappeared out of it altogether! When Lazarus resurrected, he was still wrapped up in his linen cloths and handkerchief; he was still bound and limited. When the Lord resurrected, He left the linen cloths and the handkerchief behind. This means that He transcended all barriers. The Lord's resurrection was fundamentally different from Lazarus's resurrection....God has exalted Him to the highest, and He has given Him a name that is above all names, not only in this age but in the age to come (Eph. 1:20-21). Our Christ has transcended everything in resurrection. (*The Collected Works of Watchman Nee*, vol. 59, pp. 92-93)

Further Reading: The Collected Works of Watchman Nee, vol. 59, ch. 11; vol. 42, ch. 37

Enlightenment and inspiration:

WEEK 17 — DAY 3

Morning Nourishment

Psa. You will arise *and* have compassion on Zion, for it
102:13-14 is time to be gracious to her; the appointed time has come. For Your servants take pleasure in her stones, and show favor to her dust.
16 For Jehovah has built up Zion; He has appeared in His glory.

The history of Israel is a picture of the history of the church. Israel passed through a time of destruction and devastation, and the people of Israel were captured and carried away to captivity in Babylon. Likewise, in the book of Revelation we see that Babylon the Great is versus the church. Eventually, Babylon the Great will fall, and the church will be fully established. That rebuilding of the church will turn all the nations to the Lord, and the kingdom of the world will become the kingdom of God and of Christ (Rev. 11:15).

Psalm 102 unveils Christ's death and His existence in His resurrection. The product of Christ's death and resurrection is Zion with God's house and God's city. Therefore, in Psalm 102 we have Christ's death, Christ's resurrection, and Zion. (*Life-study of the Psalms*, pp. 417)

Today's Reading

Zion is a total title of the church. Galatians 4:26 says that the "Jerusalem above" is our mother, and Hebrews 12:22 tells us that we have come to "Mount Zion and to the city of the living God, the heavenly Jerusalem." Furthermore, in...[Psalm 84:5] we saw that the "highways to Zion"...are the highways of the church life. Revelation 14 shows us that the one hundred and forty-four thousand will be raptured to Mount Zion. Today we are heading to Zion, the highest peak of God's mountains. This Zion is the church.

Israel is a type of the church....Joshua, Judges, and Ruth...are a record of the history of God's elect. From our point of view this record is unpleasant, even a tragedy. From God's point of view, however, this record is pleasant because even among the devastated elect of God, there was still something on earth for God, and as long as God can have something for Himself on earth, He is satisfied. The principle is the same with the church today. The proper church life has been fully devastated, and everywhere we can see Babylon the Great. But God still has something on earth for Himself. This is the Lord's recovery.

Today, in spite of the degradation and devastation of the church, God still has a line that is for Christ, and for this we should worship Him.....Zion is the center of the city Jerusalem (Psa. 102:16, 21), typifying the church as the center of God's kingdom (Matt. 16:18-19).

In [Psalm 102:14] the stones typify the believers as the building materials of the church (1 Pet. 2:5), and the dust, the soil, typifies the ground of the church. Do you take pleasure in all the members of the church? Do you favor the ground of the church? We should be happy with all the members of the church, and we should care for the ground of the church.

Psalm 102:21 and 22 say, "That the name of Jehovah may be declared in Zion, / And His praise, in Jerusalem, / When the peoples are gathered together, / And the kingdoms, to serve Jehovah." These verses indicate that it is through the established, restored Zion—the church—that all the nations and kingdoms will be brought into the praise and worship of Jehovah. This means that the church turns the world to the Lord.

Christ is the key that turns the earth to the Lord because of His eternal and unchanging existence (vv. 24-27; Heb. 1:10-12). Christ died and resurrected, and now He lives forever in His resurrection. Christ's existence is unchanging throughout all the generations because of His resurrection.

Christ's death produced the church. The church has been devastated and will be restored. Christ's resurrection then will enable the church to continue its existence. (*Life-study of the Psalms*, pp. 417, 420-421)

Further Reading: The Conclusion of the New Testament, msgs. 73-74; *The Glorious Church*, ch. 2

Enlightenment and inspiration: _____

WEEK 17 — DAY 4

Morning Nourishment

Eph. And what is the surpassing greatness of His power
1:19-20 toward us who believe, according to the operation of the might of His strength, which He caused to operate in Christ in raising Him from the dead and seating Him at His right hand in the heavenlies.

Psalm 102 is very deep, containing some hidden secrets. If we have insight into this psalm, we will see that Christ's suffering and death are not only for redemption but also for restoration.... Christ's suffering is for redemption, and His redemption is to produce the church as the house of God and the city of God, which will consummate in the restoration. It is in,...by,...and through Christ's resurrection that the church will consummate in the restoration. Christ's death produced the church, and His resurrection prolongs the existence of the church. Having been produced through Christ's death, the church has its continued existence in Christ's resurrection. (*Life-study of the Psalms*, pp. 417-418)

Today's Reading

After Christ terminated the entire old creation through His all-inclusive death, the church was produced in His resurrection (1 Pet. 1:3; Eph. 2:6). The church is an entity absolutely in resurrection; it is not natural, nor is it of the old creation. The church is a new creation created in Christ's resurrection and by the resurrected Christ....We must also see where the church is. The church today is in Christ in ascension. Ephesians 2:6 tells us that the church has been resurrected with Christ, and now the church is seated in the heavenlies with Christ. Therefore, the church is absolutely and purely of the element of Christ, absolutely in resurrection, and absolutely remaining in the heavenlies with Christ. (*Elders' Training, Book 2: The Vision of the Lord's Recovery*, pp. 37-38)

As a type of Christ, the lampstand portrays Christ as the resurrection life growing, branching, budding, and blossoming to shine the light....Since the lampstand typifies Christ, it indicates that Christ is the One who is growing. Remember that the lampstand is not made up of only one branch and one lamp. On the contrary, as the central stalk grows, it produces three pairs of branches. Moreover, all the branches are growing and have knobs, buds, and blossoms....Christ grows first in Himself and then also in us as the branches. (*Life-study of Exodus*, p. 1097)

The Body of Christ could not come forth from the incarnated Christ until He had been crucified to terminate the flesh, the natural man, and the entire old creation. After terminating all these things through His crucifixion, Christ entered into resurrection to germinate something new. Therefore, it was after His resurrection that the Body of Christ came into being. In our natural life and in the old creation we are not the Body. But we are the Body in the new creation germinated by Christ's resurrection life. (*The Conclusion of the New Testament*, pp. 2098-2099)

Jesus is the embodiment of God, and God is the Spirit. So, in the universe the Holy Spirit, the consummated Spirit, the life-giving Spirit, is the reality of resurrection. God is resurrection; Christ is resurrection. Hence, wherever God is and wherever Christ is, there is resurrection. Eventually, the consummated Spirit is resurrection. When we live in the Spirit, we live in resurrection. (*The Issue of the Union of the Consummated Spirit of the Triune God and the Regenerated Spirit of the Believers*, p. 15)

We must realize that the sevenfold intensified life-giving Spirit only honors things in resurrection. If you do any work which is not in resurrection, the life-giving Spirit will never honor it. Thus, your labor will be in vain, with no result. Most of the work in today's Christianity is not in resurrection. Most Christians work in their natural life, not by the divine and mystical life in resurrection. Anything that is natural belongs to the old creation. Our contact with people should not be in the old creation but in resurrection. It is only in this way that we can cherish and nourish people with Christ, the all-inclusive One. (*The Vital Groups*, p. 104)

Further Reading: Elders' Training, Book 2: The Vision of the Lord's Recovery, ch. 3; Life-study of Exodus, msg. 94

Enlightenment and inspiration:

WEEK 17 — DAY 5

Morning Nourishment

2 Cor. 1:9 Indeed we ourselves had the response of death in ourselves, that we should not base our confidence on ourselves but on God, who raises the dead.

Phil. 3:10 To know Him and the power of His resurrection and the fellowship of His sufferings, being conformed to His death.

A great part of the believers in the local churches are still in the natural man, but to be in the reality of the Body of Christ, we need to be absolutely in the resurrection life of Christ. We do have some good coordination in the local churches. However, I would ask, "Is this kind of coordination carried out by the natural life or in resurrection?" To be in resurrection means that our natural life is crucified, and then the God-created part of our being is uplifted in resurrection to be one with Christ in resurrection....We all need to be conformed to the death of Christ by the power of His resurrection [Phil. 3:10]. We all need to ask ourselves whether the coordination among us is by the power of Christ's resurrection or merely by our natural man. (*The Practical Points concerning Blending*, pp. 19-20)

Today's Reading

We cannot see much of the reality of the Body of Christ in resurrection, that is, in the Spirit, in the pneumatic Christ, and in the consummated God. So there is the need for us to endeavor to be absolutely in the resurrection life of Christ....[and] to reach in the church life the highest peak, today's Zion, of the reality of the Body of Christ until we consummate in the New Jerusalem, including Zion.

Paul said, "I am crucified with Christ; and it is no longer I who live, but it is Christ who lives in me" (Gal. 2:20a). This is not an exchange, because Paul went on to say, "And the life which I now live in the flesh I live in faith, the faith of the Son of God..." (v. 20b). Paul was a person living not by himself but by the pneumatic Christ, and this pneumatic Christ is the all-inclusive Spirit, who is the consummation of the processed and consummated Triune God. All of this is in resurrection. When you do not live by your natural life, but live by the divine life within you, you are in resurrection. The issue of this is the Body of Christ. The reality of the divine life within us is the resurrection, which is the pneumatic Christ, the all-inclusive Spirit, and the processed and consummated Triune God. (*The Practical Points concerning Blending*, pp. 20, 27)

The natural strength and ability are useful if they are dealt with by the cross. After being dealt with by the cross, they are in resurrection....In resurrection something divine has been wrought into our strength and ability....After being dealt with, our strength and ability become useful in resurrection for our service to the Lord. (*Basic Lessons on Service*, pp. 155-156)

The English language does not give us adequate adjective forms for the nouns Christ and resurrection. We must, therefore, invent some new vocabulary words to communicate such a vision of the church. We may say that today the church is "Christly," "resurrectionly," and heavenly. These three adjectives describe the fact conveyed in the Bible. The church is of Christ; the church is of resurrection; the church is of the heavens. The church is Christly, resurrectionly, and heavenly. (*Elders' Training, Book 2: The Vision of the Lord's Recovery*, p. 38)

[Acts 2:24 says], "Whom God has raised up, having loosed the pangs of death, since it was not possible for Him to be held by it." Death cannot hold Him. Once all those who are alive go into death, they cannot come out again, but the Lord Jesus cannot be held by death. Death has no strength to hold Him. This is resurrection. His life can endure death; therefore, the principle of resurrection in the Bible becomes very precious. "Who became dead and lived again" [Rev. 2:8] proves that life can endure death. God sees the church as a being that can endure death. The gates of Hades are open to the church, but the gates of Hades cannot prevail against her and cannot confine her; thus, the nature of the church is resurrection....That which passes through death and still remains is resurrection. (*The Orthodoxy of the Church*, pp. 21-22)

Further Reading: Words of Life from the 1988 Full-time Training, chs. 4-6; *The Experience of Life*, ch. 11

Enlightenment and inspiration: _____

WEEK 17 — DAY 6

Morning Nourishment

Rev. 1:18 And the living One; and I became dead, and behold, I am living forever and ever; and I have the keys of death and of Hades.

Eph. 1:22-23 And He subjected all things under His feet and gave Him *to be* Head over all things to the church, which is His Body, the fullness of the One who fills all in all.

The church is where the Lord is the Head and we are the Body. What is the relationship between the church and resurrection, and what is the relationship between the church and the Holy Spirit? Ephesians 1:19-20 speaks of the surpassing greatness of His power which God caused to operate in Christ. The church is the place where God demonstrates the operation of the might of His strength, according to the power which He caused to operate in Christ. (*The Collected Works of Watchman Nee*, vol. 59, p. 86)

Today's Reading

We have to pay attention to the words *according to* [in v. 19]. They mean that God is causing the same degree of might and strength that operated in Christ to now operate in the church. Those who have might do not necessarily have strength, and those who have strength do not necessarily have might, but here we have "the might of His strength."...The church can now experience the same might and strength that the Lord experienced. The church is the same as the resurrected Lord not only in nature but also in power. If this were not so, everything about the church would be vanity. Just as God broke through all barriers in the Lord, He is breaking through all barriers in the church. Therefore, the church should be the same as the resurrected Lord. It should be as powerful, as free, and as unfettered by any limitation as the Lord is. Otherwise, it cannot be called the church. The might of God's strength not only operated in Christ, but it continually operates in the church as well. Today the church is the depository and storehouse of the power of resurrection. This is the church. Anything less than this will not do. The church is the Body of Christ. Therefore, this might and strength cannot be anything less than they should be....Today the church has received this power supply from the ascended and glorified Christ.....It is no less than the very power that operated in Christ. When the Lord was on the earth, there was no church, because Christ was not yet resurrected; everything was bound. The church was produced after Christ rose from the dead, ascended to the height, and poured forth the Holy Spirit. The church became the Body of Christ after the Lord's resurrection. The church is filled with all that He is; it is the very vessel which holds the resurrected Christ. This is the meaning of the church.

Today the church is the depository of the resurrection power of Christ. What is the Holy Spirit doing today? He is manifesting the resurrection power of Christ through the church. All the problems are over now. The Lord said that the gates of Hades cannot prevail against the church. Personally, I believe that the gates here refer to all the gates of Hades. They are all open to the church, and they cannot prevail against the church because Hades represents death, and the church represents resurrection. This is the reason the church is victorious. Whether or not the Lord has a way on earth today is not a matter of changing our behavior or knowing some truth. Some must be ready to pay the price to know resurrection, to know the Holy Spirit, and to know the church. When we know these things, the church will have a glorious testimony. (*The Collected Works of Watchman Nee*, vol. 59, pp. 86-88)

According to the New Testament, Christ has had two births. His first birth took place at His incarnation, and His second birth was in His resurrection. The church came into being through the resurrection of Christ. In His second birth the firstborn Son of God was born with all His brothers, who are the members of His Body, the church. Therefore, the church was born in resurrection, that is, in the second birth of Christ. The church now continues its existence in the all-inclusive Spirit. (*Life-study of Colossians*, p. 221)

Further Reading: The Collected Works of Watchman Nee, vol. 59, ch. 10; *Life-study of Ephesians*, msgs. 16-17

Enlightenment and inspiration: _____

WEEK 17 — HYMN

Hymns, #1176

1 Pow'r exceeding great God did demonstrate
   When He raised His Son from the dead.
   May this pow'r we see, with it strengthened be,
   And in resurrection life be led.

   Power, power, resurrection power,
   Energize us mightily within!
   Power, power, resurrection power,
   Energize us in the inner man!

2 Pow'r exceeding high God did magnify
   When He raised His Son far above all.
   Principalities, pow'rs, and majesties
   At the name of Jesus Christ must fall.

   Power, power, all-transcending power,
   Elevate us mightily within!
   Power, power, all-transcending power,
   Elevate us in the inner man!

3 Pow'r surpassing too, all things to subdue
   Has been given to Christ, pow'r complete.
   We His Body are; so, hallelujah,
   Everything must be beneath our feet!

   Power, power, all-subduing power,
   All-subjecting mightily within!
   Power, power, all-subduing power,
   All-subjecting to the inner man!

4 And the best of all, overruling all,
   O'er all to the church Christ is Head.
   Pow'r so glorious over all's *to us;*
   To the highest place the church is led.

   Power, power, overruling power,
   Ruling over all, without, within!
   Power, power, overruling power,
   Ruling, reigning, through the inner man!

WEEK 17 — PROPHECY

Composition for prophecy with main point and sub-points:

WEEK 18 — OUTLINE

The Highest Revelation of Christ

Scripture Reading: Psa. 110

Day 1

I. **God has made Christ to sit at His right hand (Psa. 110:1-2):**
   A. "Jehovah declares to my Lord,/Sit at My right hand/Until I make Your enemies/Your footstool" (v. 1):
      1. This word, which concerns Christ in His ascension, has been quoted directly more than twenty times in the New Testament and has been quoted indirectly approximately another twenty times (cf. Matt. 22:44; Mark 12:36; 16:19; Luke 20:42-43; Acts 2:33-35; Rom. 8:34; Heb. 1:13).
      2. The Lord Jesus quoted this verse to reveal His divinity as the Lord of David (Matt. 22:41-46).
      3. The highest place in the universe is at the right hand of God (cf. Ezek. 47:1).
      4. Christ's ascension to the right hand of God is not merely a matter of His being in a place but of His being in a person, the Father; in His ascension Christ entered into the Father's being and sat down there (Heb. 1:3b; John 16:28).
      5. This word about Christ's sitting at the right hand of God implies Christ's kingship (Psa. 80:17; Col. 1:17a, 18b; Rev. 22:1; Ezek. 1:22, 26; cf. Isa. 14:13; 3 John 9; 1 John 5:21).
      6. In His ascension Christ was made by God the Lord, the Christ, the Leader of the entire universe, and the Savior (Acts 2:36; 5:31; 10:36).
      7. Christ is on the throne, but He is still in need of a footstool:
         a. God is endeavoring to subdue all of Christ's enemies and to make them His footstool.
         b. Our fighting today is for the subduing of Christ's enemies (Rom. 5:17, 21).

WEEK 18 — OUTLINE

B. God will send forth from Zion the scepter of Christ's strength to rule over all the nations at His return (Psa. 110:2).

Day 2

II. We need to cooperate with Christ's heavenly ministry in the day of His warfare by presenting ourselves as freewill offerings to the Lord in the splendor of consecration and by being His young men who are to Him like the dew from the womb of the dawn (v. 3):

A. In the eyes of the Lord our willing consecration, our offering ourselves to Him, is a matter of splendor:
   1. Although the church has become degraded, throughout the centuries there has been a line of those who have offered themselves willingly to the Lord in the splendor, the beauty, of their consecration.
   2. *Splendor* may also be translated "adornment"; the splendor of consecration is an adornment; if we offer ourselves willingly to the Lord, we will be beautified with a divine, heavenly splendor.

B. Here Christ likens Himself to a plant that needs the watering of the mild, soft, gentle dew:
   1. As Christ is on the way to carry out God's economy, He needs to be watered; Christ is watered by those who offer themselves willingly to Him.
   2. Whoever volunteers himself to Christ as an offering is a young man likened to the dew conceived in the womb of the dawn for watering Christ.

Day 3

C. In order to cooperate with Christ's heavenly ministry in the day of His warfare, we need to have an absolute and thorough consecration to the Lord of our whole being with everything that we have for the accomplishment of His eternal economy; the fullness of one's experience of life depends on the fullness of one's experience of consecration (Matt. 26:6-13):

WEEK 18 — OUTLINE

1. The basis of consecration is God's purchase (1 Cor. 6:19-20; Rom. 14:8).
2. The motive of consecration is God's love (2 Cor. 5:14-15; Rom. 12:1).
3. The meaning of consecration is to be a sacrifice (v. 1; Num. 28:2-3).
4. The purpose of consecration is to let God work in us so that we might work for God (Eph. 2:10; Isa. 64:8; Phil. 2:12-13; 1 Cor. 15:10).
5. The result of consecration is to abandon our future (Lev. 1:9; cf. 6:10-13).

D. In order to cooperate with Christ's heavenly ministry in the day of His warfare, we need to rise up early in the morning to contact the Lord so that we may enter into the womb of the dawn to be conceived as the dew for Christ's watering (Matt. 6:6; 14:22-23; Mark 1:35).

E. In order to cooperate with Christ's heavenly ministry in the day of His warfare, we need to live a life of the altar and the tent, keeping ourselves empty, open, fresh, living, and young with the Lord for His new move (Gen. 12:7-8):
   1. We need to be emptied and unloaded in our spirit, in the depth of our being, so that we may receive Christ as the reality of the kingdom of the heavens (Matt. 5:3; Luke 1:53).
   2. We need to be open vessels; the one who experiences the greatest amount of transformation is the one who is the most open to the Lord (18:17; Prov. 20:27; Rev. 4:5).
   3. We need to receive the Spirit as the fresh oil (Zech. 4:12-14; Matt. 25:8-9; Rev. 3:18).
   4. We need to walk in newness of life and serve in newness of spirit (Rom. 6:4; 7:6; cf. Ezek. 36:26-27; 2 Cor. 3:16; Matt. 5:8; 26:29).
   5. We need to be vitalized by the Lord to be the living and functioning members of His Body (1 Cor. 14:4b, 31; cf. Rev. 3:1; 14:4).

Day 4

WEEK 18 — OUTLINE

6. We need to be renewed day by day with the fresh supply of the resurrection life to stay young in the Lord (2 Cor. 4:16; Eph. 5:26-27).

Day 5

F. In order to cooperate with Christ's heavenly ministry in the day of His warfare, we need to fight for the brothers in oneness with Him to cherish the churches in His humanity and nourish the churches in His divinity to produce the overcomers through His organic shepherding (Gen. 14:13-20; Rev. 1:13; 2:7; 1 Pet. 5:4; Heb. 13:20; 1 John 5:16; cf. Acts 6:4; Rev. 1:20).

III. **God has sworn and will not change in ordaining Christ a Priest forever according to the order of Melchizedek (Psa. 110:4; Heb. 5:6, 10):**

A. Christ is not only the King with power and authority (Psa. 110:1-2) but also the High Priest (Heb. 2:17; 4:14; 6:20; 8:1; 9:11):
   1. Christ's heavenly ministry in His ascension includes both His kingship and His priesthood (7:1-2; Zech. 6:13).
   2. As the King, He has the scepter to rule over the earth and to manage our affairs, and as the High Priest, He is interceding for us and taking care of our case before God (Heb. 4:14-16; 7:25-26; 9:24; Rom. 8:34; Rev. 1:12-13).

B. As the kingly High Priest according to the order of Melchizedek, Christ ministers God into us as our supply to fulfill God's eternal purpose (Heb. 7:1-2; 8:1-2; Gen. 14:18):
   1. In His earthly ministry Christ was a High Priest according to the order of Aaron for the putting away of sin (Heb. 9:14, 26).
   2. Then, in His heavenly ministry Christ was designated a High Priest according to the order of Melchizedek (5:6, 10), not to offer sacrifices for sin but to minister to us the very God who was processed through incarnation, human living, crucifixion, and resurrection, signified by the bread and the wine (Matt.

26:26-28), as our life supply so that we may be saved to the uttermost (Heb. 7:25).
  C. As the High Priest, Christ cherishes the churches in His humanity and nourishes them in His divinity with His divine love (Rev. 1:12-13; 2:1).

Day 6
IV. **Christ, who is the Lord *(Adonai)* and who is at God's right hand, will shatter kings in the day of His anger at His coming back with His overcomers and will execute judgment among the nations over a great land (Psa. 110:5-6; Dan. 2:34-35, 44; Joel 3:11-12; Rev. 17:14):**
  A. This indicates that Christ is the Warrior to be the greatest Victor, overcoming all the nations, shattering the kings and the head of the enemies, and executing judgment upon all who oppose Him (Psa. 2:9, 12; Dan. 2:44; Rev. 2:26-27).
  B. He will come with His bride, a composition of all His overcomers, as His army, and with her He will fight against and defeat Antichrist and his armies (19:11-21).

V. **Christ will drink from the brook by the way and will lift up His head triumphantly (Psa. 110:7):**
  A. The brook signifies the overcomers; as Christ is taking the lead to fight through to the end, He will need water to drink, and this water will be the overcomers.
  B. Christ's lifting up His head is a sign of His victory, His triumph, in overcoming all the enemies.
  C. To the enemies Christ is the Victor, but to us He is the Drinker.
  D. In this psalm we see Christ as the King, the Priest, the Warrior, the Victor, and the Drinker (the Coming One).

WEEK 18 — DAY 1

Morning Nourishment

Psa. 110:1-2 **Jehovah declares to my Lord, Sit at My right hand until I make Your enemies Your footstool. Jehovah will send forth the scepter of Your strength from Zion: Rule in the midst of Your enemies.**

In Psalm 109, within the saints in their suffering, we have the cry of Christ to God (cf. Psa. 109:8; Acts 1:20). In Psalm 110 we see the answer, God's answer, to Christ's cry. This answer is exceedingly high—not deep but high. Martin Luther said that this psalm is the greatest of all the psalms. In a sense, I agree with him. It has only seven verses, just as Psalm 87, that wonderful psalm regarding the city. Psalm 110, however, is not about the city but about Christ in the city. It is divided into four sections: (1) the first three verses, (2) verse 4, (3) verses 5 and 6, and (4) verse 7. (*Christ and the Church Revealed and Typified in the Psalms,* p. 188)

Although Psalm 110 is one of the shortest of the psalms, it is the highest revelation of Christ....[Verse 1a] which concerns Christ in His ascension (Heb. 1:3b), has been quoted directly more than twenty times in the New Testament and has been quoted indirectly approximately another twenty times. Again and again the New Testament refers to this word concerning Christ in His ascension. (*Life-study of the Psalms,* p. 432)

Today's Reading

Christ is God; in His divinity He is the Lord of David. He is also a man; in His humanity He is the son of David. The Pharisees had only half the scriptural knowledge concerning Christ's person, that is, that He was the son of David according to His humanity. They did not have the other half, that is, that He was the Son of God according to His divinity. (Matt. 22:45, footnote 1)

The highest place in the universe is the right hand of God. Let us use as an illustration the desire of a child to be in his mother's arms, at her bosom. You may offer a child the best seat in a palace, but he will not care to be in that place if his mother is not there. The child might say, "I don't want to be in that place—

I want to be in the arms of my mother." To the child, the best place, the highest place, is in his mother's arms, at her bosom. In like manner, Christ's ascension is not merely a matter of His being in a place but of His being in a person, the Father. In His ascension Christ entered into the Father's being and sat down there.

This word [in Psalm 110:1] about Christ's sitting at the right hand of God implies Christ's kingship. In the New Testament we are told that in His ascension Christ has been made by God the Lord, the Christ, the Leader of the entire universe, and the Savior (Acts 2:36; 5:31; 10:36). This concerns Christ's kingship.

According to Psalm 110:1, Christ is sitting at God's right hand until God makes Christ's enemies His footstool. At home you may have an excellent seat, but you may not have a footstool. Likewise, Christ is on the throne, but He is still in need of a footstool. Thus, God is endeavoring to subdue all of Christ's enemies and to make them His footstool. Our fighting today is for the subduing of Christ's enemies.

Zion [in verse 2] is not the Zion on earth but the Zion in the heavens, as mentioned in Hebrews 12 and Revelation 14. Hebrews 12:22 says that we have "come forward to Mount Zion and to the city of the living God, the heavenly Jerusalem." Revelation 14:1-5 shows us that the living overcomers will be raptured to Zion in the heavens. From this heavenly Zion God will send out the scepter of Christ's power to rule over all the nations. The word "enemies" in Psalm 110:2 refers to the nations. Today the nations are His enemies. For example, in their way of dealing with Israel, the Arab nations are the enemies of Christ. (*Life-study of the Psalms*, pp. 432-433)

When God has secured Zion in a full way, Christ will return. Then, out of Zion, God will send forth the scepter of Christ's strength to rule over all the nations. The day will come. (*Christ and the Church Revealed and Typified in the Psalms*, p. 189)

Further Reading: Christ and the Church Revealed and Typified in the Psalms, ch. 19; *The Conclusion of the New Testament*, msgs. 74-76

Enlightenment and inspiration: _____

WEEK 18 — DAY 2

Morning Nourishment

Psa. Your people will offer themselves willingly in the
110:3 day of Your warfare, in the splendor of *their* consecration. Your young men will be to You like the dew from the womb of the dawn.

Judg. ...The leaders took the lead in Israel,...the people
5:2 have willingly offered themselves, Bless Jehovah.

Literally, the Hebrew words translated "offer themselves willingly" [in Psalm 110:3] mean "be freewill offerings." [The word *warfare* indicates] that some kind of fighting is raging on. Today is still a time of fighting because Christ still does not have a footstool. Hence, this ministry is engaged in a constant struggle. We stand against and annul every kind of improper ground concerning the church, whether Catholic or Protestant, and this causes opposition and fighting.

In the day of His warfare, or army, Christ's people will offer themselves willingly "in the splendor of their consecration."...In the eyes of the Lord our willing consecration...is a kind of splendor. Although the church has become degraded, throughout the centuries there has been a line of those who have offered themselves willingly to the Lord in the splendor, the beauty, of their consecration.(*Life-study of the Psalms*, pp. 433-434)

Today's Reading

Giving up everything on earth, thousands have offered themselves freely to Christ, and with this offering there was the splendor of consecration. John Nelson Darby was such a person. Darby lived to be eighty-four years of age and, because of his love for Christ, he never married. One day, in his old age, he was staying alone in a hotel and he said, "Lord Jesus, I still love You." No doubt, Darby was a freewill offering to the Lord in the splendor of consecration.

Instead of the word "splendor" some versions use the word "adornment." The splendor of consecration is an adornment. We need to be adorned by offering ourselves willingly to the Lord. If we do this, we will be beautified with a divine, heavenly splendor.

[Psalm 110:3b] indicates that, on the one hand, Christ likes to see the splendor of our consecration; on the other hand, He desires the dew that comes from the womb of the dawn. Christ enjoys seeing the splendor of those who offer themselves to Him as freewill offerings, but, even more important, He still needs some dew to water Him….He needs us to be the dew that waters Him.

According to the poetry here, this dew comes from "the womb of the dawn." We need to enter into this womb to be conceived as the dew with which to water Christ. I believe that this involves the morning watch. If we do not rise up early in the morning, we will miss the opportunity to enter into the womb of the morning to be made dew for Christ's watering. Instead of being watered, He will be dry and we also will be dry. I hope that we all, especially the young people, will see that here Christ likens Himself to a plant that needs the mild, soft, gentle dew. May we respond to Him by saying, "Lord Jesus, I want to be the dew conceived and produced by the womb of the morning for You to be watered." (*Life-study of the Psalms,* pp. 434-435)

Here Christ likens Himself to a plant that needs the watering of the mild, soft, gentle dew. As Christ is on His way to carry out God's economy, He needs to be watered. Christ is watered by those who offer themselves willingly to Him. Whoever volunteers himself to Christ as an offering is a young man likened to the dew conceived in the womb of the dawn for watering Christ. (Psa. 110:3, footnote 3)

We are the dew to Him in the morning, and we are the brook to Him in the daytime, while He is on His way to fight with the enemy.…Christ is riding on and riding through triumphantly, and on His way…He needs all of us, as a kind of refreshment to Him. We are the dew and the refreshing water to Christ so that He may lift up His head. (*Christ and the Church Revealed and Typified in the Psalms,* p. 191)

Further Reading: Consecration; Messages for Building Up New Believers, vol. 1, ch. 3

Enlightenment and inspiration:

WEEK 18 — DAY 3

Morning Nourishment

Gen. **And Jehovah appeared to Abram and said, To your**
12:7-8 **seed I will give this land....There he built an altar to Jehovah who had appeared to him. And he proceeded from there to the mountain on the east of Bethel and pitched his tent,...and there he built an altar to Jehovah and called upon the name of Jehovah.**

Concerning the experience of consecration there are five main points: the basis of consecration, the motive of consecration, the meaning of consecration, the purpose of consecration, and the result of consecration....Consecration is not just a knowing of the right of ownership in the mind or a feeling of love in our affections, nor is it only an attitude and expression of ours toward God. Actually speaking, consecration itself is...a major part of life. The experience of consecration, therefore, is really the experience of life. The fullness of one's experience of life depends on the fullness of one's experience of consecration. Hence, if one pursues the experience of consecration, it will enable him to grow in life. (*The Experience of Life*, pp. 29, 47-48)

Today's Reading

Since consecration is a part of life, then by following this life and living in this life, the law of life will cause the five points of consecration to be clearly and spontaneously worked out in us. When we first consecrate ourselves, our experience is similar to an embryo in the mother's womb—one cannot distinguish the ear, the eye, the mouth, and the nose. As we grow in life, however, these five points related to the experience of consecration gradually become formed in us. Then we really have a feeling that we have been bought by God and that all our rights are in His hand. We become a prisoner of His love because His love has pierced our hearts. We become a sacrifice indeed, laid on the altar for God's enjoyment and satisfaction. We will be those who have been thoroughly worked over by God and are then able to work for Him. Our future will truly be as a handful of ashes. All our ways of escape outside of God's will shall have been cut off; God only will be our future and our way. At that time the experience of our consecration will indeed have become matured. (*The Experience of Life,* p. 48)

The life of a Christian is the life of the altar and the tent. The altar is toward God while the tent is toward the world. In His presence, God requires that His children have an altar and on the earth that they have a tent....God appeared to Abraham, and Abraham built an altar. This altar was not for a sin offering but for a burnt offering. A sin offering is for redemption, while a burnt offering is an offering of ourselves to God. The altar [here] does not refer to the Lord Jesus' vicarious death for us; it refers to the consecration of ourselves to God. It was the kind of altar spoken of in Romans 12:1: "I exhort you therefore, brothers, through the compassions of God to present your bodies a living sacrifice, holy, well pleasing to God, which is your reasonable service." (*The Life of the Altar and the Tent,* pp. 1, 4)

An altar is for worshipping God by offering all that we are and have to God for His purpose. Abraham's building of an altar was motivated by God's reappearing and can be considered an anti-testimony to the building of the tower of Babel. (Gen. 12:7, footnote 3)

Abraham first built an altar for the worship of God; then he pitched a tent for his living. Abraham, Isaac, and Jacob each lived in a tent (Gen. 12:8; 26:25; 35:21). Their dwelling in tents was a declaration that they were strangers and sojourners on the earth who were seeking a better country and eagerly waiting for "the city which has the foundations, whose Architect and Builder is God" (Heb. 11:9-10, 13-16). Both the better country and the city which has the foundations are the New Jerusalem. (Gen. 12:8, footnote 2)

To be poor in spirit is not only to be humble but also to be emptied in our spirit, in the depth of our being, not holding on to the old things of the old dispensation but unloaded to receive the new things, the things of the kingdom of the heavens. (Matt. 5:3, footnote 2)

Further Reading: The Experience of Life, ch. 3; *The Life of the Altar and the Tent*

Enlightenment and inspiration: _____
_____
_____
_____

Morning Nourishment

Rom. We have been buried therefore with Him through
6:4 baptism into His death, in order that just as Christ was raised from the dead through the glory of the Father, so also we might walk in newness of life.

7:6 ...We serve in newness of spirit and not in oldness of letter.

2 Cor. ...Though our outer man is decaying, yet our inner
4:16 *man* is being renewed day by day.

Who experiences the greatest amount of transformation? It is the one who is absolutely open to the Lord. "Lord, I am fully open to You. I want to keep opening to You. My whole being is open—my heart, my mind, my will, and my emotions. Keep shining. Search me thoroughly. Enlighten and enliven me. I will accept it fully." In this way, the light will penetrate into every area, and life simultaneously will be supplied to you. The man of clay will be transformed into the image of Christ. As the gold is thus formed in you, there will be the seven Spirits shining forth and manifesting God....As we are enlightened by the lamps within us, we shall become the golden lampstand in reality in our locality, manifesting the Triune God. Then He will have His testimony. (*Life Messages*, vol. 2, pp. 248-249)

Today's Reading

In [Zechariah] 3 and 4 the same person, Zerubbabel, is signified by a shoot (3:8), a tree (4:3, 11), and a branch (v. 12). This indicates that Zerubbabel himself is not the source....Christ is the unique olive tree...and all Christ's believers are branches, shoots, of Christ (John 15:5a). Thus, all the believers are the many olive trees, not in the sense of being separate trees but in the sense of being branches of Christ, the unique olive tree.

Which [in Zechariah 4:12] refers not to the spouts but to the branches. For the shining of the lampstand, oil is needed....The oil denotes the Spirit, and the Spirit is God, who in typology is signified by gold. Thus, to supply the oil for the shining of the lampstand is to flow out God to supply others with the sevenfold Spirit that they may be enlivened for God's testimony through the church. (Zech. 4:12, footnotes 1, 2, and 3)

In [Romans] 6:4, newness of life issues from our being identified with Christ's resurrection and is for our walk in our daily life. [In 7:6] newness of spirit issues from our being discharged from the law and being joined to the resurrected Christ, and is for our service to God. Thus, both newness of spirit and newness of life are results of the crucifixion of the old man.

[The word *spirit* in 7:6 refers] to our regenerated human spirit, in which the Lord as the Spirit dwells (2 Tim. 4:22). Everything that is related to our regenerated spirit is new, and everything that comes out of our spirit is new. Our regenerated spirit is a source of newness because the Lord, the life of God, and the Holy Spirit are there. (Rom. 7:6, footnotes 3 and 4)

The recovery needs to be vital today. The recovery needs a revival of morale,...of impact,...of the dynamic motivation within us,...[and] of vitality among us....We are still not vital. We are still in our habit, still somewhat in our tradition. We need to be vitalized.

After a person is gained and baptized, he must be raised up to be a living member of the Body of Christ. Today what God needs are...living members so that His Body can be built up to the fullest extent....God is not satisfied until every saved and baptized one is a living member who can be useful for the building up of the Body of Christ. (*1993 Blending Conference Messages concerning the Lord's Recovery and Our Present Need,* pp. 143-144, 154)

[We are being renewed] by being nourished with the fresh supply of the resurrection life. As our mortal body, our outer man, is being consumed by the killing work of death, our inner man, that is, our regenerated spirit with the inward parts of our being...is being metabolically renewed day by day with the supply of the resurrection life. (2 Cor. 4:16, footnote 3)

Further Reading: The Vital Groups, msgs. 2-3; *Life Messages,* vol. 2, ch. 69

Enlightenment and inspiration: _____

WEEK 18 — DAY 5

Morning Nourishment

Psa. 110:4 Jehovah has sworn, and He will not change: You are a Priest forever according to the order of Melchizedek.

Heb. 7:1 For this Melchizedek, king of Salem, priest of the Most High God, who met Abraham returning from the slaughter of the kings and blessed him.

Our Christ today is our High Priest. In His humanity...He sympathizes with our weakness because He was tempted in all respects like us....Meanwhile, He is nourishing us in His divinity with all the positive aspects of His person....He is taking care of the churches in the recovery in both ways. In His humanity He is cherishing us to make us proper so that we may be happy, pleasant, and comfortable. In His divinity He is nourishing us so that we may grow and mature in the divine life to be His overcomers to accomplish His eternal economy. (*The Vital Groups*, p. 109)

Today's Reading

Christ is not only the King with power and authority, as indicated in Psalm 110:2; He is also the High Priest, as revealed in verse 4. Today we need Christ not only as our King but also as our Priest to pray for us and to take care of our case before God.

The first section [of Christ's ministry] was His ministry on earth, and the second section is His ministry in the heavens. In His earthly ministry He did many things. Now,...Christ in His ascension is carrying out the second, the heavenly, section of His ministry. This includes both His kingship and His priesthood. As the King He has the scepter signifying power and authority to rule over the earth and to manage our affairs, and as the High Priest He is praying for us and taking care of our case. (*Life-study of the Psalms*, p. 435)

Melchizedek [in Genesis 14:18] is a type of Christ as the kingly High Priest....After Abraham gained the victory, Melchizedek appeared. Before his appearing, Melchizedek, a priest of God, must have been interceding for Abraham. It must have been through his intercession that Abraham was able to slaughter the four kings and gain the victory (cf. Exo. 17:8-13). Today Christ, our High Priest, is interceding for us in a hidden way (Rom. 8:34b; Heb. 7:25b) that we may be His overcomers to defeat God's enemies, so that through our victory Christ can be manifested openly in His second coming.

The priesthood according to the order of Melchizedek is higher than the Aaronic priesthood (Heb. 7). In His earthly ministry Christ was a High Priest according to the order of Aaron for the putting away of sin (Heb. 9:14, 26). Then, in His heavenly ministry Christ was designated a High Priest according to the order of Melchizedek (Heb. 5:6, 10), not to offer sacrifices for sin but to minister to us the very God who was processed through incarnation, human living, crucifixion, and resurrection, signified by the bread and the wine (Matt. 26:26-28), as our life supply that we may be saved to the uttermost (Heb. 7:25a). (Gen. 14:18, footnotes 1 and 3)

As the King of righteousness (Isa. 32:1), Christ made all things right with God and made all things right with one another. Righteousness issues in peace (Isa. 32:17). As the King of peace (Isa. 9:6), Christ, through righteousness, brings in peace between God and us, and in such a peace He fulfills the ministry of His priesthood. He is the King who becomes the Priest; thus, His priesthood is kingly, royal (1 Pet. 2:9). (Heb. 7:1, footnote 2)

At the beginning of [Hebrews 7] we have the King, and at the end we have the Son of God (v. 28), indicating that Christ as our High Priest is both kingly and divine. His kingship maintains a condition that is full of righteousness and peace that He may minister the processed Triune God to us for our enjoyment; His divinity as the Son of God constitutes Him a High Priest who is living and full of life that He may be able to continue His priesthood perpetually. (Heb. 7:2, footnote 1)

Further Reading: The Vital Groups, msgs. 10-11; *Life-study of Hebrews,* msg. 28; *Life-study of Genesis,* msg. 43

Enlightenment and inspiration: _____

_____

_____

WEEK 18 — DAY 6

Morning Nourishment

Psa. 110:5-7 The Lord is at Your right hand; He will shatter kings in the day of His anger. He will execute judgment among the nations; He will fill *the place* with corpses; He will shatter the head over a great land. He will drink from the brook by the way; therefore He will lift up *His* head.

The words "great land" [in Psalm 110:6] refer to the entire earth, the whole globe. Here we see that Christ, who is the Lord, the Master (*Adonai*), and who is at God's right hand, will shatter kings in the day of His anger at His coming back and will execute judgment among the nations (2:9, 12; Dan. 2:44; Rev. 2:26-27). This indicates that Christ will be the greatest Victor, overcoming all the nations, shattering the kings and the head of the enemies, and executing judgment upon all who oppose Him. In addition to being the King and the Priest, Christ is the Warrior to be the greatest Victor. According to Revelation 19, in His coming back He will be the fighting One. However, He will not fight alone against Antichrist and his armies from the nations. Rather, He will come with His bride, a composition of all His overcomers, as His army, and with her He will fight against Antichrist and his armies. (*Life-study of the Psalms,* p. 436)

Today's Reading

"He will drink from the brook by the way; / Therefore He will lift up His head" (Psa. 110:7). While Christ is fighting, He will be thirsty. Needing some water to drink, He will drink from "the brook by the way." This brook is the overcomers. Those who offer themselves in the splendor of consecration are the dew of the morning to water Christ, and the overcomers are the brook to quench His thirst. As Christ is taking the lead to fight through to the end, He will need water to drink, and this water will be the overcomers. I believe that this interpretation is correct because it fits in with the New Testament teaching.

When Christ drinks from the brook, "He will lift up His head." This means that He will be victorious. To lower our head is a sign of defeat, but to lift up our head is a sign of victory, of triumph. Those who lift up their head are the ones who overcome all the enemies.

To the enemies Christ is the Victor, but to us He is a Drinker. We may say to Him, "Hallelujah! Lord Jesus, You are the Victor." But He may say to us, "Yes, I am the Victor, but to you I would like to be the Drinker." In this psalm we see Christ as the King, the Priest, the Warrior, the Victor, and the Drinker. Christ overcomes the enemies, and He drinks from the overcomers, from the brook by the way. (*Life-study of the Psalms*, pp. 436-437)

He needs both the dew in the morning and the fresh water by the way. "Therefore He will lift up His head." What is this water of the brook from which Christ drinks? Do not forget that this is poetry. According to the context of the entire psalm, the brook mentioned here must be the saints. While Christ is on His way, while He is fighting through to defeat His enemies, He needs refreshment; He needs a living fountain. He is our living water, and we are His drink. He is our refreshment, and we are His refreshment. We are the dew to Him in the morning, and we are the brook to Him in the daytime, while He is on His way to fight with the enemy. I do believe deeply within my spirit that this is right. Christ is riding on and riding through triumphantly, and on His way He needs you, He needs me, He needs all of us, as a kind of refreshment to Him. We are the dew and the refreshing water to Christ so that He may lift up His head. Are you willing to be as the dew and as the brook? (*Christ and the Church Revealed and Typified in the Psalms*, p. 191)

Further Reading: Life-study of the Psalms, msg. 38; Life-study of Revelation, msg. 55

Enlightenment and inspiration: _____

WEEK 18 — HYMN

Hymns, #1102

1. The Lord said unto my Lord,
   "Sit Thou at My right hand;
   Thy foes shall be Thy footstool,
   Upon them Thou shalt stand."
   The sceptre of Thy strength shall
   The Lord from Zion send
   To rule o'er all the nations
   Forever 'til the end.

2. A voluntary offering,
   The young ones are to Thee;
   In consecration's splendor
   How beautiful to see!
   For as the dew of morning
   Refreshes all the land —
   The young ones given to Thee
   Are precious in Thy hand.

3. The Lord hath sworn forever
   And never will turn back,
   "Thou art a priest forever,
   As was Melchizedek."
   Oh, Thou hast no beginning
   Of days; of life: no end!
   And on Thine intercession
   We ever do depend.

4. The Lord is at Thy right hand
   And in His day of wrath
   He'll strike through rulers, judging
   The nations in His path.
   While riding on to triumph
   He'll drink of us, the stream,
   His head uplifted, strengthened,
   The whole earth to redeem.

5. Oh Lord, Thou art ascended
   To God's right hand to sit;
   As Head o'er all things, to Thee
   God doth Thy foes commit.
   Our King — for us Thou reignest,
   Our Priest — we are supplied,
   Our all we give unto Thee,
   Thou Conqueror glorified.

WEEK 18 — PROPHECY

Composition for prophecy with main point and sub-points: _____

Reading Schedule for the Recovery Version of the Old Testament with Footnotes

Wk.	Lord's Day	Monday	Tuesday	Wednesday	Thursday	Friday	Saturday
1	☐ Gen 1:1-5	☐ 1:6-23	☐ 1:24-31	☐ 2:1-9	☐ 2:10-25	☐ 3:1-13	☐ 3:14-24
2	☐ 4:1-26	☐ 5:1-32	☐ 6:1-22	☐ 7:1—8:3	☐ 8:4-22	☐ 9:1-29	☐ 10:1-32
3	☐ 11:1-32	☐ 12:1-20	☐ 13:1-18	☐ 14:1-24	☐ 15:1-21	☐ 16:1-16	☐ 17:1-27
4	☐ 18:1-33	☐ 19:1-38	☐ 20:1-18	☐ 21:1-34	☐ 22:1-24	☐ 23:1—24:27	☐ 24:28-67
5	☐ 25:1-34	☐ 26:1-35	☐ 27:1-46	☐ 28:1-22	☐ 29:1-35	☐ 30:1-43	☐ 31:1-55
6	☐ 32:1-32	☐ 33:1—34:31	☐ 35:1-29	☐ 36:1-43	☐ 37:1-36	☐ 38:1—39:23	☐ 40:1—41:13
7	☐ 41:14-57	☐ 42:1-38	☐ 43:1-34	☐ 44:1-34	☐ 45:1-28	☐ 46:1-34	☐ 47:1-31
8	☐ 48:1-22	☐ 49:1-15	☐ 49:16-33	☐ 50:1-26	☐ Exo 1:1-22	☐ 2:1-25	☐ 3:1-22
9	☐ 4:1-31	☐ 5:1-23	☐ 6:1-30	☐ 7:1-25	☐ 8:1-32	☐ 9:1-35	☐ 10:1-29
10	☐ 11:1-10	☐ 12:1-14	☐ 12:15-36	☐ 12:37-51	☐ 13:1-22	☐ 14:1-31	☐ 15:1-27
11	☐ 16:1-36	☐ 17:1-16	☐ 18:1-27	☐ 19:1-25	☐ 20:1-26	☐ 21:1-36	☐ 22:1-31
12	☐ 23:1-33	☐ 24:1-18	☐ 25:1-22	☐ 25:23-40	☐ 26:1-14	☐ 26:15-37	☐ 27:1-21
13	☐ 28:1-21	☐ 28:22-43	☐ 29:1-21	☐ 29:22-46	☐ 30:1-10	☐ 30:11-38	☐ 31:1-17
14	☐ 31:18—32:35	☐ 33:1-23	☐ 34:1-35	☐ 35:1-35	☐ 36:1-38	☐ 37:1-29	☐ 38:1-31
15	☐ 39:1-43	☐ 40:1-38	☐ Lev 1:1-17	☐ 2:1-16	☐ 3:1-17	☐ 4:1-35	☐ 5:1-19
16	☐ 6:1-30	☐ 7:1-38	☐ 8:1-36	☐ 9:1-24	☐ 10:1-20	☐ 11:1-47	☐ 12:1-8
17	☐ 13:1-28	☐ 13:29-59	☐ 14:1-18	☐ 14:19-32	☐ 14:33-57	☐ 15:1-33	☐ 16:1-17
18	☐ 16:18-34	☐ 17:1-16	☐ 18:1-30	☐ 19:1-37	☐ 20:1-27	☐ 21:1-24	☐ 22:1-33
19	☐ 23:1-22	☐ 23:23-44	☐ 24:1-23	☐ 25:1-23	☐ 25:24-55	☐ 26:1-24	☐ 26:25-46
20	☐ 27:1-34	☐ Num 1:1-54	☐ 2:1-34	☐ 3:1-51	☐ 4:1-49	☐ 5:1-31	☐ 6:1-27
21	☐ 7:1-41	☐ 7:42-88	☐ 7:89—8:26	☐ 9:1-23	☐ 10:1-36	☐ 11:1-35	☐ 12:1—13:33
22	☐ 14:1-45	☐ 15:1-41	☐ 16:1-50	☐ 17:1—18:7	☐ 18:8-32	☐ 19:1-22	☐ 20:1-29
23	☐ 21:1-35	☐ 22:1-41	☐ 23:1-30	☐ 24:1-25	☐ 25:1-18	☐ 26:1-65	☐ 27:1-23
24	☐ 28:1-31	☐ 29:1-40	☐ 30:1—31:24	☐ 31:25-54	☐ 32:1-42	☐ 33:1-56	☐ 34:1-29
25	☐ 35:1-34	☐ 36:1-13	☐ Deut 1:1-46	☐ 2:1-37	☐ 3:1-29	☐ 4:1-49	☐ 5:1-33
26	☐ 6:1—7:26	☐ 8:1-20	☐ 9:1-29	☐ 10:1-22	☐ 11:1-32	☐ 12:1-32	☐ 13:1—14:21

Reading Schedule for the Recovery Version of the Old Testament with Footnotes

Wk.	Lord's Day	Monday	Tuesday	Wednesday	Thursday	Friday	Saturday
27	14:22—15:23	16:1-22	17:1—18:8	18:9—19:21	20:1—21:17	21:18—22:30	23:1-25
28	24:1-22	25:1-19	26:1-19	27:1-26	28:1-68	29:1-29	30:1—31:29
29	31:30—32:52	33:1-29	34:1-12	Josh 1:1-18	2:1-24	3:1-17	4:1-24
30	5:1-15	6:1-27	7:1-26	8:1-35	9:1-27	10:1-43	11:1—12:24
31	13:1-33	14:1—15:63	16:1—18:28	19:1-51	20:1—21:45	22:1-34	23:1—24:33
32	Judg 1:1-36	2:1-23	3:1-31	4:1-24	5:1-31	6:1-40	7:1-25
33	8:1-35	9:1-57	10:1—11:40	12:1—13:25	14:1—15:20	16:1-31	17:1—18:31
34	19:1-30	20:1-48	21:1-25	Ruth 1:1-22	2:1-23	3:1-18	4:1-22
35	1 Sam 1:1-28	2:1-36	3:1—4:22	5:1—6:21	7:1—8:22	9:1-27	10:1—11:15
36	12:1—13:23	14:1-52	15:1-35	16:1-23	17:1-58	18:1-30	19:1-24
37	20:1-42	21:1—22:23	23:1—24:22	25:1-44	26:1-25	27:1—28:25	29:1—30:31
38	31:1-13	2 Sam 1:1-27	2:1-32	3:1-39	4:1—5:25	6:1-23	7:1-29
39	8:1—9:13	10:1—11:27	12:1-31	13:1-39	14:1-33	15:1—16:23	17:1—18:33
40	19:1-43	20:1—21:22	22:1-51	23:1-39	24:1-25	1 Kings 1:1-19	1:20-53
41	2:1-46	3:1-28	4:1-34	5:1—6:38	7:1-22	7:23-51	8:1-36
42	8:37-66	9:1-28	10:1-29	11:1-43	12:1-33	13:1-34	14:1-31
43	15:1-34	16:1—17:24	18:1-46	19:1-21	20:1-43	21:1—22:53	2 Kings 1:1-18
44	2:1—3:27	4:1-44	5:1—6:33	7:1-20	8:1-29	9:1-37	10:1-36
45	11:1—12:21	13:1—14:29	15:1-38	16:1-20	17:1-41	18:1-37	19:1-37
46	20:1—21:26	22:1-20	23:1-37	24:1—25:30	1 Chron 1:1-54	2:1—3:24	4:1—5:26
47	6:1-81	7:1-40	8:1-40	9:1-44	10:1—11:47	12:1-40	13:1—14:17
48	15:1—16:43	17:1-27	18:1—19:19	20:1—21:30	22:1—23:32	24:1—25:31	26:1-32
49	27:1-34	28:1—29:30	2 Chron 1:1-17	2:1—3:17	4:1—5:14	6:1-42	7:1—8:18
50	9:1—10:19	11:1—12:16	13:1—15:19	16:1—17:19	18:1—19:11	20:1-37	21:1—22:12
51	23:1—24:27	25:1—26:23	27:1—28:27	29:1-36	30:1—31:21	32:1-33	33:1—34:33
52	35:1—36:23	Ezra 1:1-11	2:1-70	3:1—4:24	5:1—6:22	7:1-28	8:1-36

Reading Schedule for the Recovery Version of the Old Testament with Footnotes

Wk.	Lord's Day	Monday	Tuesday	Wednesday	Thursday	Friday	Saturday
53	9:1—10:44	Neh 1:1-11	2:1—3:32	4:1—5:19	6:1-19	7:1-73	8:1-18
54	9:1-20	9:21-38	10:1—11:36	12:1-47	13:1-31	Esth 1:1-22	2:1—3:15
55	4:1—5:14	6:1—7:10	8:1-17	9:1—10:3	Job 1:1-22	2:1—3:26	4:1—5:27
56	6:1—7:21	8:1—9:35	10:1—11:20	12:1—13:28	14:1—15:35	16:1—17:16	18:1—19:29
57	20:1—21:34	22:1—23:17	24:1—25:6	26:1—27:23	28:1—29:25	30:1—31:40	32:1—33:33
58	34:1—35:16	36:1-33	37:1-24	38:1-41	39:1-30	40:1-24	41:1-34
59	42:1-17	Psa 1:1-6	2:1—3:8	4:1—6:10	7:1—8:9	9:1—10:18	11:1—15:5
60	16:1—17:15	18:1-50	19:1—21:13	22:1-31	23:1—24:10	25:1—27:14	28:1—30:12
61	31:1—32:11	33:1—34:22	35:1—36:12	37:1-40	38:1—39:13	40:1—41:13	42:1—43:5
62	44:1-26	45:1-17	46:1—48:14	49:1—50:23	51:1—52:9	53:1—55:23	56:1—58:11
63	59:1—61:8	62:1—64:10	65:1—67:7	68:1-35	69:1—70:5	71:1—72:20	73:1—74:23
64	75:1—77:20	78:1-72	79:1—81:16	82:1—84:12	85:1—87:7	88:1—89:52	90:1—91:16
65	92:1—94:23	95:1—97:12	98:1—101:8	102:1—103:22	104:1—105:45	106:1-48	107:1-43
66	108:1—109:31	110:1—112:10	113:1—115:18	116:1—118:29	119:1-32	119:33-72	119:73-120
67	119:121-176	120:1—124:8	125:1—128:6	129:1—132:18	133:1—135:21	136:1—138:8	139:1—140:13
68	141:1—144:15	145:1—147:20	148:1—150:6	Prov 1:1-33	2:1—3:35	4:1—5:23	6:1-35
69	7:1—8:36	9:1—10:32	11:1—12:28	13:1—14:35	15:1-33	16:1-33	17:1-28
70	18:1-24	19:1—20:30	21:1—22:29	23:1-35	24:1—25:28	26:1—27:27	28:1—29:27
71	30:1-33	31:1-31	Eccl 1:1-18	2:1—3:22	4:1—5:20	6:1—7:29	8:1—9:18
72	10:1—11:10	12:1-14	S.S 1:1-8	1:9-17	2:1-17	3:1-11	4:1-8
73	4:9-16	5:1-16	6:1-13	7:1-13	8:1-14	Isa 1:1-11	1:12-31
74	2:1-22	3:1-26	4:1-6	5:1-30	6:1-13	7:1-25	8:1-22
75	9:1-21	10:1-34	11:1—12:6	13:1-22	14:1-14	14:15-32	15:1—16:14
76	17:1—18:7	19:1-25	20:1—21:17	22:1-25	23:1-18	24:1-23	25:1-12
77	26:1—21	27:1-13	28:1-29	29:1-24	30:1-33	31:1—32:20	33:1-24
78	34:1-17	35:1-10	36:1-22	37:1-38	38:1—39:8	40:1-31	41:1-29

Reading Schedule for the Recovery Version of the Old Testament with Footnotes

Wk.	Lord's Day	Monday	Tuesday	Wednesday	Thursday	Friday	Saturday
79	☐ 42:1-25	☐ 43:1-28	☐ 44:1-28	☐ 45:1-25	☐ 46:1-13	☐ 47:1-15	☐ 48:1-22
80	☐ 49:1-13	☐ 49:14-26	☐ 50:1—51:23	☐ 52:1-15	☐ 53:1-12	☐ 54:1-17	☐ 55:1-13
81	☐ 56:1-12	☐ 57:1-21	☐ 58:1-14	☐ 59:1-21	☐ 60:1-22	☐ 61:1-11	☐ 62:1-12
82	☐ 63:1-19	☐ 64:1-12	☐ 65:1-25	☐ 66:1-24	☐ Jer 1:1-19	☐ 2:1-19	☐ 2:20-37
83	☐ 3:1-25	☐ 4:1-31	☐ 5:1-31	☐ 6:1-30	☐ 7:1-34	☐ 8:1-22	☐ 9:1-26
84	☐ 10:1-25	☐ 11:1—12:17	☐ 13:1-27	☐ 14:1-22	☐ 15:1-21	☐ 16:1—17:27	☐ 18:1-23
85	☐ 19:1—20:18	☐ 21:1—22:30	☐ 23:1-40	☐ 24:1—25:38	☐ 26:1—27:22	☐ 28:1—29:32	☐ 30:1-24
86	☐ 31:1-23	☐ 31:24-40	☐ 32:1-44	☐ 33:1-26	☐ 34:1-22	☐ 35:1-19	☐ 36:1-32
87	☐ 37:1-21	☐ 38:1-28	☐ 39:1—40:16	☐ 41:1—42:22	☐ 43:1—44:30	☐ 45:1—46:28	☐ 47:1—48:16
88	☐ 48:17-47	☐ 49:1-22	☐ 49:23-39	☐ 50:1-27	☐ 50:28-46	☐ 51:1-27	☐ 51:28-64
89	☐ 52:1-34	☐ Lam 1:1-22	☐ 2:1-22	☐ 3:1-39	☐ 3:40-66	☐ 4:1-22	☐ 5:1-22
90	☐ Ezek 1:1-14	☐ 1:15-28	☐ 2:1—3:27	☐ 4:1—5:17	☐ 6:1—7:27	☐ 8:1—9:11	☐ 10:1—11:25
91	☐ 12:1—13:23	☐ 14:1—15:8	☐ 16:1-63	☐ 17:1—18:32	☐ 19:1-14	☐ 20:1-49	☐ 21:1-32
92	☐ 22:1-31	☐ 23:1-49	☐ 24:1-27	☐ 25:1—26:21	☐ 27:1-36	☐ 28:1-26	☐ 29:1—30:26
93	☐ 31:1—32:32	☐ 33:1-33	☐ 34:1-31	☐ 35:1—36:21	☐ 36:22-38	☐ 37:1-28	☐ 38:1—39:29
94	☐ 40:1-27	☐ 40:28-49	☐ 41:1-26	☐ 42:1—43:27	☐ 44:1-31	☐ 45:1-25	☐ 46:1-24
95	☐ 47:1-23	☐ 48:1-35	☐ Dan 1:1-21	☐ 2:1-30	☐ 2:31-49	☐ 3:1-30	☐ 4:1-37
96	☐ 5:1-31	☐ 6:1-28	☐ 7:1-12	☐ 7:13-28	☐ 8:1-27	☐ 9:1-27	☐ 10:1-21
97	☐ 11:1-22	☐ 11:23-45	☐ 12:1-13	☐ Hosea 1:1-11	☐ 2:1-23	☐ 3:1—4:19	☐ 5:1-15
98	☐ 6:1-11	☐ 7:1-16	☐ 8:1-14	☐ 9:1-17	☐ 10:1-15	☐ 11:1-12	☐ 12:1-14
99	☐ 13:1—14:9	☐ Joel 1:1-20	☐ 2:1-16	☐ 2:17-32	☐ 3:1-21	☐ Amos 1:1-15	☐ 2:1-16
100	☐ 3:1-15	☐ 4:1—5:27	☐ 6:1—7:17	☐ 8:1—9:15	☐ Obad 1-21	☐ Jonah 1:1-17	☐ 2:1—4:11
101	☐ Micah 1:1-16	☐ 2:1—3:12	☐ 4:1—5:15	☐ 6:1—7:20	☐ Nahum 1:1-15	☐ 2:1—3:19	☐ Hab 1:1-17
102	☐ 2:1-20	☐ 3:1-19	☐ Zeph 1:1-18	☐ 2:1-15	☐ 3:1-20	☐ Hag 1:1-15	☐ 2:1-23
103	☐ Zech 1:1-21	☐ 2:1-13	☐ 3:1-10	☐ 4:1-14	☐ 5:1—6:15	☐ 7:1—8:23	☐ 9:1-17
104	☐ 10:1—11:17	☐ 12:1—13:9	☐ 14:1-21	☐ Mal 1:1-14	☐ 2:1-17	☐ 3:1-18	☐ 4:1-6

Reading Schedule for the Recovery Version of the New Testament with Footnotes

Wk.	Lord's Day	Monday	Tuesday	Wednesday	Thursday	Friday	Saturday
1	Matt 1:1-2	1:3-7	1:8-17	1:18-25	2:1-23	3:1-6	3:7-17
2	4:1-11	4:12-25	5:1-4	5:5-12	5:13-20	5:21-26	5:27-48
3	6:1-8	6:9-18	6:19-34	7:1-12	7:13-29	8:1-13	8:14-22
4	8:23-34	9:1-13	9:14-17	9:18-34	9:35—10:5	10:6-25	10:26-42
5	11:1-15	11:16-30	12:1-14	12:15-32	12:33-42	12:43—13:2	13:3-12
6	13:13-30	13:31-43	13:44-58	14:1-13	14:14-21	14:22-36	15:1-20
7	15:21-31	15:32-39	16:1-12	16:13-20	16:21-28	17:1-13	17:14-27
8	18:1-14	18:15-22	18:23-35	19:1-15	19:16-30	20:1-16	20:17-34
9	21:1-11	21:12-22	21:23-32	21:33-46	22:1-22	22:23-33	22:34-46
10	23:1-12	23:13-39	24:1-14	24:15-31	24:32-51	25:1-13	25:14-30
11	25:31-46	26:1-16	26:17-35	26:36-46	26:47-64	26:65-75	27:1-26
12	27:27-44	27:45-56	27:57—28:15	28:16-20	Mark 1:1	1:2-6	1:7-13
13	1:14-28	1:29-45	2:1-12	2:13-28	3:1-19	3:20-35	4:1-25
14	4:26-41	5:1-20	5:21-43	6:1-29	6:30-56	7:1-23	7:24-37
15	8:1-26	8:27—9:1	9:2-29	9:30-50	10:1-16	10:17-34	10:35-52
16	11:1-16	11:17-33	12:1-27	12:28-44	13:1-13	13:14-37	14:1-26
17	14:27-52	14:53-72	15:1-15	15:16-47	16:1-8	16:9-20	Luke 1:1-4
18	1:5-25	1:26-46	1:47-56	1:57-80	2:1-8	2:9-20	2:21-39
19	2:40-52	3:1-20	3:21-38	4:1-13	4:14-30	4:31-44	5:1-26
20	5:27—6:16	6:17-38	6:39-49	7:1-17	7:18-23	7:24-35	7:36-50
21	8:1-15	8:16-25	8:26-39	8:40-56	9:1-17	9:18-26	9:27-36
22	9:37-50	9:51-62	10:1-11	10:12-24	10:25-37	10:38-42	11:1-13
23	11:14-26	11:27-36	11:37-54	12:1-12	12:13-21	12:22-34	12:35-48
24	12:49-59	13:1-9	13:10-17	13:18-30	13:31—14:6	14:7-14	14:15-24
25	14:25-35	15:1-10	15:11-21	15:22-32	16:1-13	16:14-22	16:23-31
26	17:1-19	17:20-37	18:1-14	18:15-30	18:31-43	19:1-10	19:11-27

Reading Schedule for the Recovery Version of the New Testament with Footnotes

Wk.	Lord's Day	Monday	Tuesday	Wednesday	Thursday	Friday	Saturday
27	Luke 19:28-48 ☐	20:1-19 ☐	20:20-38 ☐	20:39—21:4 ☐	21:5-27 ☐	21:28-38 ☐	22:1-20 ☐
28	22:21-38 ☐	22:39-54 ☐	22:55-71 ☐	23:1-43 ☐	23:44-56 ☐	24:1-12 ☐	24:13-35 ☐
29	24:36-53 ☐	John 1:1-13 ☐	1:14-18 ☐	1:19-34 ☐	1:35-51 ☐	2:1-11 ☐	2:12-22 ☐
30	2:23—3:13 ☐	3:14-21 ☐	3:22-36 ☐	4:1-14 ☐	4:15-26 ☐	4:27-42 ☐	4:43-54 ☐
31	5:1-16 ☐	5:17-30 ☐	5:31-47 ☐	6:1-15 ☐	6:16-31 ☐	6:32-51 ☐	6:52-71 ☐
32	7:1-9 ☐	7:10-24 ☐	7:25-36 ☐	7:37-52 ☐	7:53—8:11 ☐	8:12-27 ☐	8:28-44 ☐
33	8:45-59 ☐	9:1-13 ☐	9:14-34 ☐	9:35—10:9 ☐	10:10-30 ☐	10:31—11:4 ☐	11:5-22 ☐
34	11:23-40 ☐	11:41-57 ☐	12:1-11 ☐	12:12-24 ☐	12:25-36 ☐	12:37-50 ☐	13:1-11 ☐
35	13:12-30 ☐	13:31-38 ☐	14:1-6 ☐	14:7-20 ☐	14:21-31 ☐	15:1-11 ☐	15:12-27 ☐
36	16:1-15 ☐	16:16-33 ☐	17:1-5 ☐	17:6-13 ☐	17:14-24 ☐	17:25—18:11 ☐	18:12-27 ☐
37	18:28-40 ☐	19:1-16 ☐	19:17-30 ☐	19:31-42 ☐	20:1-13 ☐	20:14-18 ☐	20:19-22 ☐
38	20:23-31 ☐	21:1-14 ☐	21:15-22 ☐	21:23-25 ☐	Acts 1:1-8 ☐	1:9-14 ☐	1:15-26 ☐
39	2:1-13 ☐	2:14-21 ☐	2:22-36 ☐	2:37-41 ☐	2:42-47 ☐	3:1-18 ☐	3:19—4:22 ☐
40	4:23-37 ☐	5:1-16 ☐	5:17-32 ☐	5:33-42 ☐	6:1—7:1 ☐	7:2-29 ☐	7:30-60 ☐
41	8:1-13 ☐	8:14-25 ☐	8:26-40 ☐	9:1-19 ☐	9:20-43 ☐	10:1-16 ☐	10:17-33 ☐
42	10:34-48 ☐	11:1-18 ☐	11:19-30 ☐	12:1-25 ☐	13:1-12 ☐	13:13-43 ☐	13:44—14:5 ☐
43	14:6-28 ☐	15:1-12 ☐	15:13-34 ☐	15:35—16:5 ☐	16:6-18 ☐	16:19-40 ☐	17:1-18 ☐
44	17:19-34 ☐	18:1-17 ☐	18:18-28 ☐	19:1-20 ☐	19:21-41 ☐	20:1-12 ☐	20:13-38 ☐
45	21:1-14 ☐	21:15-26 ☐	21:27-40 ☐	22:1-21 ☐	22:22-29 ☐	22:30—23:11 ☐	23:12-15 ☐
46	23:16-30 ☐	23:31—24:21 ☐	24:22—25:5 ☐	25:6-27 ☐	26:1-13 ☐	26:14-32 ☐	27:1-26 ☐
47	27:27—28:10 ☐	28:11-22 ☐	28:23-31 ☐	Rom 1:1-2 ☐	1:3-7 ☐	1:8-17 ☐	1:18-25 ☐
48	1:26—2:10 ☐	2:11-29 ☐	3:1-20 ☐	3:21-31 ☐	4:1-12 ☐	4:13-25 ☐	5:1-11 ☐
49	5:12-17 ☐	5:18—6:5 ☐	6:6-11 ☐	6:12-23 ☐	7:1-12 ☐	7:13-25 ☐	8:1-2 ☐
50	8:3-6 ☐	8:7-13 ☐	8:14-25 ☐	8:26-39 ☐	9:1-18 ☐	9:19—10:3 ☐	10:4-15 ☐
51	10:16—11:10 ☐	11:11-22 ☐	11:23-36 ☐	12:1-3 ☐	12:4-21 ☐	13:1-14 ☐	14:1-12 ☐
52	14:13-23 ☐	15:1-13 ☐	15:14-33 ☐	16:1-5 ☐	16:6-24 ☐	16:25-27 ☐	1 Cor 1:1-4 ☐

Reading Schedule for the Recovery Version of the New Testament with Footnotes

Wk.	Lord's Day	Monday	Tuesday	Wednesday	Thursday	Friday	Saturday
53	1 Cor 1:5-9	1:10-17	1:18-31	2:1-5	2:6-10	2:11-16	3:1-9
54	3:10-13	3:14-23	4:1-9	4:10-21	5:1-13	6:1-11	6:12-20
55	7:1-16	7:17-24	7:25-40	8:1-13	9:1-15	9:16-27	10:1-4
56	10:5-13	10:14-33	11:1-6	11:7-16	11:17-26	11:27-34	12:1-11
57	12:12-22	12:23-31	13:1-13	14:1-12	14:13-25	14:26-33	14:34-40
58	15:1-19	15:20-28	15:29-34	15:35-49	15:50-58	16:1-9	16:10-24
59	2 Cor 1:1-4	1:5-14	1:15-22	1:23—2:11	2:12-17	3:1-6	3:7-11
60	3:12-18	4:1-6	4:7-12	4:13-18	5:1-8	5:9-15	5:16-21
61	6:1-13	6:14—7:4	7:5-16	8:1-15	8:16-24	9:1-15	10:1-6
62	10:7-18	11:1-15	11:16-33	12:1-10	12:11-21	13:1-10	13:11-14
63	Gal 1:1-5	1:6-14	1:15-24	2:1-13	2:14-21	3:1-4	3:5-14
64	3:15-22	3:23-29	4:1-7	4:8-20	4:21-31	5:1-12	5:13-21
65	5:22-26	6:1-10	6:11-15	6:16-18	Eph 1:1-3	1:4-6	1:7-10
66	1:11-14	1:15-18	1:19-23	2:1-5	2:6-10	2:11-14	2:15-18
67	2:19-22	3:1-7	3:8-13	3:14-18	3:19-21	4:1-4	4:5-10
68	4:11-16	4:17-24	4:25-32	5:1-10	5:11-21	5:22-26	5:27-33
69	6:1-9	6:10-14	6:15-18	6:19-24	Phil 1:1-7	1:8-18	1:19-26
70	1:27—2:4	2:5-11	2:12-16	2:17-30	3:1-6	3:7-11	3:12-16
71	3:17-21	4:1-9	4:10-23	Col 1:1-8	1:9-13	1:14-23	1:24-29
72	2:1-7	2:8-15	2:16-23	3:1-4	3:5-15	3:16-25	4:1-18
73	1 Thes 1:1-3	1:4-10	2:1-12	2:13—3:5	3:6-13	4:1-10	4:11—5:11
74	5:12-28	2 Thes 1:1-12	2:1-17	3:1-18	1 Tim 1:1-2	1:3-4	1:5-14
75	1:15-20	2:1-7	2:8-15	3:1-13	3:14—4:5	4:6-16	5:1-25
76	6:1-10	6:11-21	2 Tim 1:1-10	1:11-18	2:1-15	2:16-26	3:1-13
77	3:14—4:8	4:9-22	Titus 1:1-4	1:5-16	2:1-15	3:1-8	3:9-15
78	Philem 1:1-11	1:12-25	Heb 1:1-2	1:3-5	1:6-14	2:1-9	2:10-18

Reading Schedule for the Recovery Version of the New Testament with Footnotes

Wk.	Lord's Day	Monday	Tuesday	Wednesday	Thursday	Friday	Saturday
79	Heb 3:1-6	3:7-19	4:1-9	4:10-13	4:14-16	5:1-10	5:11—6:3
80	6:4-8	6:9-20	7:1-10	7:11-28	8:1-6	8:7-13	9:1-4
81	9:5-14	9:15-28	10:1-18	10:19-28	10:29-39	11:1-6	11:7-19
82	11:20-31	11:32-40	12:1-2	12:3-13	12:14-17	12:18-26	12:27-29
83	13:1-7	13:8-12	13:13-15	13:16-25	James 1:1-8	1:9-18	1:19-27
84	2:1-13	2:14-26	3:1-18	4:1-10	4:11-17	5:1-12	5:13-20
85	1 Pet 1:1-2	1:3-4	1:5	1:6-9	1:10-12	1:13-17	1:18-25
86	2:1-3	2:4-8	2:9-17	2:18-25	3:1-13	3:14-22	4:1-6
87	4:7-16	4:17-19	5:1-4	5:5-9	5:10-14	2 Pet 1:1-2	1:3-4
88	1:5-8	1:9-11	1:12-18	1:19-21	2:1-3	2:4-11	2:12-22
89	3:1-6	3:7-9	3:10-12	3:13-15	3:16	3:17-18	1 John 1:1-2
90	1:3-4	1:5	1:6	1:7	1:8-10	2:1-2	2:3-11
91	2:12-14	2:15-19	2:20-23	2:24-27	2:28-29	3:1-5	3:6-10
92	3:11-18	3:19-24	4:1-6	4:7-11	4:12-15	4:16—5:3	5:4-13
93	5:14-17	5:18-21	2 John 1:1-3	1:4-9	1:10-13	3 John 1:1-6	1:7-14
94	Jude 1:1-4	1:5-10	1:11-19	1:20-25	Rev 1:1-3	1:4-6	1:7-11
95	1:12-13	1:14-16	1:17-20	2:1-6	2:7	2:8-9	2:10-11
96	2:12-14	2:15-17	2:18-23	2:24-29	3:1-3	3:4-6	3:7-9
97	3:10-13	3:14-18	3:19-22	4:1-5	4:6-7	4:8-11	5:1-6
98	5:7-14	6:1-8	6:9-17	7:1-8	7:9-17	8:1-6	8:7-12
99	8:13—9:11	9:12-21	10:1-4	10:5-11	11:1-4	11:5-14	11:15-19
100	12:1-4	12:5-9	12:10-18	13:1-10	13:11-18	14:1-5	14:6-12
101	14:13-20	15:1-8	16:1-12	16:13-21	17:1-6	17:7-18	18:1-8
102	18:9—19:4	19:5-10	19:11-16	19:17-21	20:1-6	20:7-10	20:11-15
103	21:1	21:2	21:3-8	21:9-13	21:14-18	21:19-21	21:22-27
104	22:1	22:2	22:3-11	22:12-15	22:16-17	22:18-21	

Week 13 — Day 1

Today's verses

Psa. 74:1-2 Why, O God, have You cast *us* off forever?...Remember Your assembly, which You have purchased of old, which You have redeemed as the tribe of Your inheritance, *and* Mount Zion, where You dwell.

Jer. 2:13 For My people have committed two evils: they have forsaken Me, the fountain of living waters, to hew out for themselves cisterns, broken cisterns, which hold no water.

_____
Date

Week 13 — Day 2

Today's verses

Rev. 2:4 But I have one *thing* against you, that you have left your first love.

1 John 4:16 And we know and have believed the love which God has in us. God is love, and he who abides in love abides in God and God abides in him.

5:21 Little children, guard yourselves from idols.

_____
Date

Week 13 — Day 3

Today's verses

Psa. 73:16-17 When I considered this in order to understand *it*, it was a troublesome task in my sight, until I went into the sanctuary of God...

25-26 Whom do I have in heaven but You? And besides You there is nothing I desire on earth. My flesh and my heart fail, *but* God is the rock of my heart and my portion forever.

_____
Date

Week 13 — Day 4

Today's verses

Psa. 73:28 But as for me, drawing near to God is good for me; I have made the Lord Jehovah my refuge, that I may declare all Your works.

77:13 O God, Your way is in the sanctuary; who is so great a god as God?

Eph. 2:22 In whom you also are being built together into a dwelling place of God in spirit.

_____
Date

Week 13 — Day 5

Today's verses

Psa. 73:1 Surely God is good to Israel, to those who are pure in heart.

13 Surely I have purified my heart in vain, and I have washed my hands in innocence.

Matt. 5:8 Blessed are the pure in heart, for they shall see God.

_____
Date

Week 13 — Day 6

Today's verses

Psa. 80:1, 3 O Shepherd of Israel, give ear, You who lead Joseph like a flock; You who are enthroned *between* the cherubim, shine forth ...O God, restore us; and cause Your face to shine, and we will be saved.

14-15 O God of hosts, turn, we beseech You; look down from heaven and see, and visit this vine, even the stock which Your right hand has planted and the son whom You have strengthened for Yourself.

_____
Date

Week 14 — Day 1 Today's verses

Job 10:13 But You have hidden these things in Your heart; I know that this is with You.

Eph. 3:9 And to enlighten all *that they may see what* the economy of the mystery is, which throughout the ages has been hidden in God, who created all things.

Psa. 84:6 Passing through the valley of Baca, they make it a spring; indeed the early rain covers it with blessings.

Date _____

Week 14 — Day 2 Today's verses

Psa. 84:1-4 How lovely are Your tabernacles, O Jehovah of hosts! My soul longs, indeed even faints, for the courts of Jehovah.…At Your *two* altars even the sparrow has found a home.…Blessed are those who dwell in Your house…

Date _____

Week 14 — Day 3 Today's verses

Psa. 84:3 At Your *two* altars even the sparrow has found a home; and the swallow, a nest for herself, where she may lay her young…

Exo. 40:5-6 And you shall put the golden altar for incense before the Ark of the Testimony and set up the screen of the entrance to the tabernacle. And you shall put the altar of burnt offering before the entrance of the tabernacle of the Tent of Meeting.

Date _____

Week 14 — Day 4 Today's verses

Psa. 84:4-5 Blessed are those who dwell in Your house; they will yet be praising You. Selah. Blessed is the man whose strength is in You, in whose heart are the highways *to Zion*.
7 They go from strength to strength; *each* appears before God in Zion.

Date _____

Week 14 — Day 5 Today's verses

Psa. 84:6-7 Passing through the valley of Baca, they make it a spring; indeed the early rain covers it with blessings. They go from strength to strength; *each* appears before God in Zion.

Heb. 12:22 But you have come forward to Mount Zion and to the city of the living God, the heavenly Jerusalem; and to myriads of angels, to the universal gathering.

Date _____

Week 14 — Day 6 Today's verses

Psa. 84:10-12 For a day in Your courts is better than a thousand; I would rather stand at the threshold of the house of my God than dwell in the tents of the wicked. For Jehovah God is a sun and a shield; Jehovah gives grace and glory; He does not withhold anything good from those who walk uprightly. O Jehovah of hosts, blessed is the man who trusts in You.

Date _____

Week 15 — Day 1

Today's verses

Psa. 87:1-3   His foundation is in the holy mountains. Jehovah loves the gates of Zion more than all the dwellings of Jacob. Glorious things are spoken of you, O city of God. Selah

Date _____

Week 15 — Day 2

Today's verses

1 Cor. 3:11   For another foundation no one is able to lay besides that which is laid, which is Jesus Christ.

1:9   God is faithful, through whom you were called into the fellowship of His Son, Jesus Christ our Lord.

Date _____

Week 15 — Day 3

Today's verses

Psa. 48:1-2   Great is Jehovah, and much to be praised in the city of our God, in His holy mountain. Beautiful in elevation, the joy of the whole earth, is Mount Zion, the sides of the north, the city of the great King.

Date _____

Week 15 — Day 4

Today's verses

Psa. 87:5-6   But of Zion it will be said, This one and that one were born in her, and the Most High Himself will establish her. Jehovah will count when He records the peoples: this One was born there. Selah

Date _____

Week 15 — Day 5

Today's verses

Acts 13:33   That God has fully fulfilled this *promise* to us their children in raising up Jesus, as it is also written in the second Psalm, "You are My Son; this day have I begotten You."

Rom. 8:29   Because those whom He foreknew, He also predestinated *to be* conformed to the image of His Son, that He might be the Firstborn among many brothers.

Date _____

Week 15 — Day 6

Today's verses

Psa. 87:7   Then singing as well as dancing, *they will say*, All my springs are in you.

John 4:14   But whoever drinks of the water that I will give him shall by no means thirst forever; but the water that I will give him will become in him a fountain of water springing up into eternal life.

Date _____

Week 16 — Day 1 Today's verses

Psa. O Lord, You have been our dwelling
90:1 place in all generations.
  17 And let the favor of the Lord our God be upon us, and establish the work of our hands upon us; indeed the work of our hands, establish it.

John Abide in Me and I in you. As the branch
15:4 cannot bear fruit of itself unless it abides in the vine, so neither can you unless you abide in Me.

_____
Date

Week 16 — Day 2 Today's verses

Psa. For You have made Jehovah, who is my ref-
91:9 uge, even the Most High, Your habitation.
11-12 For He will give His angels charge concerning You to keep You in all Your ways. They will bear You up in their hands, lest You dash Your foot against a stone.

_____
Date

Week 16 — Day 3 Today's verses

Psa. You have set our iniquities before You,
90:8-10 our secret sins in the light of Your countenance....We bring our years to an end like a sigh. The days of our years are seventy years, or, if because of strength, eighty years; but their pride is labor and sorrow, for it is soon gone, and we fly away.
  12 Teach us then to number our days that we may gain a heart of wisdom.

_____
Date

Week 16 — Day 4 Today's verses

1 John And as for you, the anointing which you
2:27 have received from Him abides in you, and you have no need that anyone teach you; but as His anointing teaches you concerning all things and is true and is not a lie, and even as it has taught you, abide in Him.
  6 He who says he abides in Him ought himself also to walk even as He walked.
3:24 And he who keeps His commandments abides in Him, and He in him....

_____
Date

Week 16 — Day 5 Today's verses

1 Thes. Always rejoice, unceasingly pray, in ev-
5:16-18 erything give thanks; for this is the will of God in Christ Jesus for you.

John If you abide in Me and My words abide in
15:7 you, ask whatever you will, and it shall be done for you.

_____
Date

Week 16 — Day 6 Today's verses

Psa. But You have exalted my horn like that of
92:10 a wild ox; I am anointed with fresh oil.
12-14 The righteous man will flourish like the palm tree; he will grow like a cedar in Lebanon. Planted in the house of Jehovah, they will flourish in the courts of our God. They will still bring forth fruit in old age; they will be full of sap and green.

_____
Date

Week 17 — Day 4 Today's verses

Eph. And what is the surpassing greatness of His
1:19-20 power toward us who believe, according to the operation of the might of His strength, which He caused to operate in Christ in raising Him from the dead and seating Him at His right hand in the heavenlies.

Date _____

Week 17 — Day 5 Today's verses

2 Cor. Indeed we ourselves had the response of
1:9 death in ourselves, that we should not base our confidence on ourselves but on God, who raises the dead.

Phil. To know Him and the power of His resur-
3:10 rection and the fellowship of His sufferings, being conformed to His death.

Date _____

Week 17 — Day 6 Today's verses

Rev. And the living One; and I became dead,
1:18 and behold, I am living forever and ever; and I have the keys of death and of Hades.

Eph. And He subjected all things under His feet
1:22-23 and gave Him to be Head over all things to the church, which is His Body, the fullness of the One who fills all in all.

Date _____

Week 17 — Day 1 Today's verses

Luke And in these days He went out to the
6:12 mountain to pray, and He spent the whole night in prayer to God.

Psa. I watch, and I am like a lone sparrow on a
102:7 housetop.

Date _____

Week 17 — Day 2 Today's verses

Psa. Of old You laid the foundation of the
102:25 earth, and the heavens are the work of Your hands.

27-28 But You are the same, and Your years are without end. The children of Your servants will continue, and their seed will be established before You.

Date _____

Week 17 — Day 3 Today's verses

Psa. You will arise and have compassion on
102:13-14 Zion, for it is time to be gracious to her; the appointed time has come. For Your servants take pleasure in her stones, and show favor to her dust.

16 For Jehovah has built up Zion; He has appeared in His glory.

Date _____

Week 18 — Day 1

Today's verses

Psa. Jehovah declares to my Lord, Sit at My
110:1-2 right hand until I make Your enemies
Your footstool. Jehovah will send forth
the scepter of Your strength from Zion:
Rule in the midst of Your enemies.

Date _____

Week 18 — Day 2

Today's verses

Psa. Your people will offer themselves willingly
110:3 in the day of Your warfare, in the splendor
of *their* consecration. Your young men will
be to You like the dew from the womb of
the dawn.

Judg. …The leaders took the lead in Israel,…the
5:2 people have willingly offered themselves,
Bless Jehovah.

Date _____

Week 18 — Day 3

Today's verses

Gen. And Jehovah appeared to Abram and said,
12:7-8 To your seed I will give this land.…There he
built an altar to Jehovah who had appeared to
him. And he proceeded from there to the
mountain on the east of Bethel and pitched
his tent,…and there he built an altar to Jehovah and called upon the name of Jehovah.

Date _____

Week 18 — Day 4

Today's verses

Rom. We have been buried therefore with Him
6:4 through baptism into His death, in order
that just as Christ was raised from the dead
through the glory of the Father, so also we
might walk in newness of life.

7:6 …We serve in newness of spirit and not in
oldness of letter.

2 Cor. …Though our outer man is decaying, yet
4:16 our inner *man* is being renewed day by
day.

Date _____

Week 18 — Day 5

Today's verses

Psa. Jehovah has sworn, and He will not change:
110:4 You are a Priest forever according to the
order of Melchizedek.

Heb. For this Melchizedek, king of Salem, priest
7:1 of the Most High God, who met Abraham
returning from the slaughter of the kings
and blessed him.

Date _____

Week 18 — Day 6

Today's verses

Psa. The Lord is at Your right hand; He will
110:5-7 shatter kings in the day of His anger. He
will execute judgment among the nations; He will fill *the place* with corpses;
He will shatter the head over a great land.
He will drink from the brook by the way;
therefore He will lift up *His* head.

Date _____